Scotland the Brave?

Scotland the Brave
Independence and radical social change

Scottish Left Review Press

scottish left
review press

Published by Scottish Left Review Press
The Jimmy Reid Foundation, PO Box 8781, Biggar ML12 9AG

Scottish Left Review Press is a trading name of Left Review Scotland Ltd.,
741 Shields Road, Pollokshields, Glasgow G41 4PL

www.scottishleftreview.org

First published 2013

Copyright Gregor Gall 2013

British Library Cataloguing-in-Publication Data are available

ISBN 978-0-9550362-6-2

Printed and bound in Great Britain by:
Martins the Printers
Sea View Works
Spittal
Berwick-upon-Tweed
Northumberland TD15 1RS

Gregor Gall is professor of industrial relations at the University of Bradford. He is a columnist for the *Scotsman* and author of T*he Political Economy of Scotland: Red Scotland? Radical Scotland?*

Acknowledgement

My thanks are to Nadia Lucchesi for designing the cover and to Robin McAlpine for typesetting and production.

Scotland the Brave?

Contents

Scotland the Brave?

Summary of substantive chapters

2: Voting for the Union

Why this means a vote for either no social change or very limited social change

Radical social change is unlikely in the foreseeable future as part of the Union because of the dead hand of Westminster politics which is more abjectly colonised and controlled by forces of conservatism and neo-liberalism. Labour has shown no signs of making a significant and substantial break with the neo-liberalism of 'new' Labour, and it supports continued austerity measures. Moreover, despite a move to the left in the leadership of unions in the last decade, unions themselves remain too enfeebled to overcome these barriers and push for deep-seated social change. The sense of this is all the more acute because the referendum will not offer a second question of 'devo max' which could have envisaged further devolution of powers from Westminster to Holyrood. Now it will be a case of a simple 'yes' or 'no', with a no vote leading to the maintenance of the status quo.

3: The possibility of radical social change under independence

Independence gives greater freedom to change and facilitates heading in a progressive direction

The tangible and longstanding social democratic impulse in Scottish society – the 'red thread' and the phenomenon of 'Scottish socialism' – has become reified and reconfigured since the 1980s battle against Thatcherism into a radical form of national identity and what it means to be Scottish. However, under devolution, this has had a limited ability to gain representation in the body politic because of the maintenance of reserved business to Westminster and the conservatism of Scottish Labour. However, under independence, the SNP will fragment as its central goal has been achieved, giving rise to a new left as the SNP's left-wing joins forces with others on the left. This will also drag the Scottish Labour Party to the left. Under this reconfiguration, the left will play a far larger role in shaping society in Scotland, and significant strides towards achieving social justice can be envisaged.

4: What Scotland could look like

Seeking social justice – anything from social democracy to socialism.

Across a range of economic, political and social measures, society in Scotland can be less influenced by market mechanisms and market outcomes. Equalities of outcome can supersede 'equality of opportunity' – which in itself is something of a mirage because it operates on an unlevelled playing field. A republic of peace could exist with the an elected head of state, the withdrawal from NATO, removal of nuclear weapons from Scottish soil and Scotland could expend its current resources given over to militarism to promoting peace, not waging war. No longer would education be seen as the 'great leveller' and no longer would social mobility be relied upon for redistributing resources across families and generations. Instead, society could have a very specific set of overt principles to work by and from which policies are derived.

5: Why the SNP cannot be relied upon

Although the SNP is a left of centre party, its neoliberal economics outweigh and undermine its left stance on social issues

The SNP believes in a version of trickledown economics whereby support for capital through state aid and deregulation are believed to allow capital to grow, invest and increase profitability so that when taxed – even at a low rate – the funds for its social programme are generated. Not only is this not likely under sustained weak economic growth in the global north but past experience shows that welfare is always cut when profits fall – and falling profits are a recurring phenomenon under capitalism. In short, the SNP envisages building a Scottish version of an Irish 'tiger' economy with corporation tax at 10 %. Indeed, cutting corporation tax in this way will actually stimulate the race to the bottom with other countries as competition exists to attract the overseas investment to Scotland in the first place. So, the SNP is committed to political - not social – change but even here this is little radicalism. The monarchy and sterling will remain and defence will be part of a shared services approach with England (within NATO).

6: Red herrings

Some on the left argue independence will shatter the unity of the British working class. This is based on a misguided notion of what unity is

There is no reason why workers in Scotland will not remain in the same unions as before, that is, unions that workers in England and Wales are also members of. When the Irish state was established in 1921, the forefathers of the Unite union continued organising workers in the Republic, in the north of Ireland and in mainland Britain. The same is true of a number of other unions. The logic to remaining in the same unions is twofold. First, effectively the same companies will continue to operate north and south of the border. Second, the task is to create unions that unite workers across borders as capital operates across borders. Consequently, it is not the structures that are critical but the willingness to act collectively and for certain ends.

7: Limits to social change under independence

All Scotland's social ills cannot be resolved within Scotland because Scotland is part of a global capitalism

There are distinct limits to the extent to which 'Scottish solutions' can solve problems in Scotland because the Scottish economy is part of a capitalist world economy and subject to the same dynamics and ebbs and flows. Only some form of autarky could establish otherwise. Thus, a more full-blooded programme of social change requires that similar moves towards social liberation take place in other countries which mutually support each other and prevent the isolation of radical social experiments.

8: A boon to – not a barrier for - others

Given that the fundamental desire for independence lies in the wish to gain the ability to decide one's own destiny and to do in a progressive direction, there is no hidden or otherwise counter-position of a competitive sort towards society and citizens in England. It is not a case of the ruled and rulers in Scotland uniting to compete with the ruled and rulers in England. So there is also no reason that developments in Scotland could not become a boon to similar progressive developments in England, Wales and possibly further afield.

Chapter 1: Introduction

This book could have been called 'Imagining another Scotland', 'Another Scotland is possible' or some such allusion to the prospect of positive radical social change in the near future. But as the approach of the referendum on Thursday 18 September 2014 increasingly nears, the shrill tone of scaremongering (now dubbed 'Project Fear' by the Better Together campaign) against the case for independence has become ever greater. Stories of mild panic and much anxiety have abounded, surely signalling that phoney war since the launch of the Yes Scotland independence campaign on 26 May 2012 has come to an end and the real 'hot' war has begun. As will become clear shortly, the SNP's response to such stories and interventions has been insipid and unconvincing to say the least. Trying to strongly rebut a challenge and simultaneously take the opportunity to expound an alternative narrative and vision has not been possible because the SNP has chosen to respond within its framework of keeping the pound and the monarchy, letting the Bank of England set interest rates, staying with NATO, reducing corporation by 3% and so on. In the context of the strong attack from the forces of the Better Together campaign and the weak defence from the SNP, the title of 'Scotland the brave?' was chosen. The factors of fear and dread are in the ascendancy, with the hope of hope being continually trounced. So in the increasingly febrile atmosphere of strong anti-independence attack and weak pro-independence defence, the citizens of Scotland will need to be brave to choose not just independence but also a radical version of it.

This sets the scene for the two key tasks of this book. The first is to outline the 'what' and the 'why' of the case for a radical vision of independence for Scotland. This means what do we want independence from and what do we want independence for. The second is to outline the 'how' of that case. So, this book is about the ways and means to get to the desired goal. It has been a noticeable failure of the radical forces for independence to tackle the 'how' question. This is a critical mistake and central weakness, for it undermines the fundamental case for a radical vision of independence. To those who remain undecided, currently support the SNP's timid stance or who are on the radical left but are anti-independence, the inability or unwillingness to address the 'how' means the credibility and coherence of the 'what' and 'why' are very much undermined. The 'what' and 'why' are necessary without being sufficient on their own to win the case in the minds of citizens for independence. Adding the 'how' gives the chance of achieving critical mass and lift-off in what is already, and going to continue to be, a difficult fight. In other words, the 'how' makes the radical case for independence move from being 'necessary but insufficient' to 'necessary and sufficient'.

This is because no amount of arguing and extolling that some better world is on the near or distant horizon will do when the absence of a convincing roadmap to get there is plainly evident. This overall point about the 'how' cannot be stressed heavily enough because voting 'yes' on Saturday 18 September 2014 changes almost nothing. It will be what is done after Saturday 18 September 2014 and, in particular, as a result of the political complexion of the 2016-2020 Scottish Parliament that will be the key factors which determine more than any others what independence actually turns into. Put simply, will we have neo-liberal, capitalist independence or some form of social democratic or socialist independence? If it is to be the former, which is more than a strong possibility under the leadership of the SNP, what will be the point? Changing the Union Jack to the Saltire will not change the material welfare and well-being of the mass of citizens in Scotland one iota. But if it was to be the latter, then significant social progress could be made. Poverty and social inequality could be reduced (if not quite banished). But this will require not just the putting into Parliament of a host of progressive MSPs but also the mobilisation of citizens to put pressure on MSPs on all parties to yield to moving in a progressive direction. Radical change will take more than merely voting certain ways in both the 2014 referendum and in the 2016 Scottish Parliament elections.

In making the radical case for independence, this book pulls no punches. It argues that there is the possibility of achieving the radical case for independence and not the probability of achieving it. This is not just because the polls show that the case for independence has still yet to attain majority support but also because the forces that dominate the campaign for independence are not radical ones. Indeed, they are antipathetic to radicalism as the SNP has shown time and time again. The task then is for the radicals to not just win the case for independence per se but to also win the case for radical independence within the independence campaign and have that version as the one adopted by the mass of those voting for independence. That is a tall order which underscores the use of the language of possibility and not probability. Moreover, the project to achieve a radical form of independence will be a long and drawn out one, and one that cannot just be won within the geographical confines of Scotland. And, as will become clear, the main rationale for arguing for independence is not that it guarantees - or make probable- significant social advance but, rather, that it brings about the possibility of significant social advance several steps closer to being an actual state of affairs. This is because it will help to break the stranglehold of neo-liberalism on the political process in Britain – and of which Scotland is still subject despite devolution – by allowing for the greater expression and influence of the left of centre political compass that Scotland has.

Along the way, this book will necessarily take on the arguments from the radical left that supports the maintenance of the Union (albeit not upon the current terms that it exists). This will be done in a robust but fraternal manner because it must not be forgotten that the differences here exist primarily over the means to attain social justice and equality, rather than over ends of social justice and equality themselves. In the process, it is hoped that this contribution to the debate over independence and amongst the left can help clarify and develop our common understanding. Whatever the outcomes in 2014 and 2016, the left needs to be able to work together so fraternal, constructive debate is essential. That said, the key 'red herring' to be debunked from the anti-independence left concerns the allegation that independence will lead to the breaking up of the unity of the working class in Britain. And, of course, in doing so, the charge that the case that this book makes constitutes 'left nationalism' (as opposed to 'left internationalism') will also be dealt with.

The structure of the book is as follows. Chapter 2 'Voting for the Union' explains why a 'no' vote is a vote for either no social change or very limited social change. Chapter 3 'The possibility of radical social change under independence' argues that independence gives not just the greater freedom to create social change but also facilitates the inclination to take a certain direction towards social change. Chapter 4 'What Scotland could be like' outlines that Scotland could be about seeking social justice, namely, the move to anything from social democracy to socialism (depending on different definitions). Chapter 5 'Why the SNP cannot be relied upon' makes clear that although the SNP is a left of centre party, its neoliberal economics outweighs and undermines its left stances of social issues. Chapter 6 'Limits to social change' makes it clear that all Scotland's social ills cannot be solved within Scotland because Scotland will remain part of a globalised system of capitalism. Chapter 7 'Red Herrings' examines some of the major and misplaced objections to independence. Chapter 8 'A boon to – not a barrier for – others' further responds to the misguided and nefarious arguments from much of the left that Scottish independence will shatter the unity of the British working class and is regressive and reactionary.

Health warnings

Two health warnings are due at this point. First, the pro-independence arguments concerning the democratic rights of nations to self-determination, the abolition of the monarchy, the decentralisation of political power and the establishment of a republic as well as those concerning the blows to British imperialism and its nuclear arsenal are not dealt with in this contribution to the debate. These arguments are not unimportant but the point of this book's contribution to the debate on independence - and to support the case for independence - is to speak to a social agenda which is capable of mobilising the mass of citizens to vote for independence. Issues of the democratic right of nations, a republic and undermining British imperialism are not believed to be central to motivating most ordinary citizens to vote 'yes' on the basis of making society in Scotland fairer, more equal and justice. Common collective consciousness – as opposed to the consciousness of activists from different campaigns and groups against imperialism and militarism, for example – is far more likely to respond to those arguments that propound that an independent Scotland can see the vast majority better off in material (economic and social) terms. And while it is recognised that the progressive vision of an independent Scotland cannot be based upon one of economic growth at all costs – even assuming the fruits of the growth were fairly distributed – because of the environmental devastation that would create, this is again not an area that is touched upon for the same aforementioned reason.

The second health warning concerns whether Scotland becoming independent is economically viable. The total population of Scotland was just under 5.3m in 2011 and its Gross Domestic Project in 2011 was £127bn (or £150bn if its share of oil and gas is added). Scotland's tax revenue in 2011-2012 was £56.9bn, representing 9.8% of the UK's tax receipts whilst amounting to only 8.4% of the UK population. This would make Scotland one of the richest countries in the world. Edinburgh is the fourth largest finance centre in Europe by equity assets. In terms of as yet unrealised natural resources, there are stocks of oil and wind, wave and tidal energy supplies. These bald statistics suggest two things. On the one hand, the transition to independence is more than possible in terms of wealth and resources. Arguments to the contrary as merely disingenuous attempts to move against the case for independence. On the other hand, the pressing political issue given this munificence is one of its redistribution across the social classes in Scotland - and this is where the real contestation exists. Poverty – child poverty, the working poor, high mortality rates for adult men related to health and wealth and so on – stalks the land. There is more than enough existing and future wealth to deal with these social problems (as well as pay for the transactions costs of moving to independence). So no more than this will be said about such matters and this constitutes the second health warning because – to repeat – the purpose of this book is to make the specific argument for a particular orientation and strategy on how independence can come about. The facts and figures (about resources) to sustain the argument can freely be found elsewhere and they do not in themselves support the case for independence. While they can be supportive, to use then in this way is necessary but not sufficient to win the case for a radical form of independence. This is because it is what is done with these facts and figures and how it is done that matters and this is the concern of this book.

Chapter 2: Voting for the Union

Introduction

Radical social change is unlikely in the foreseeable future as part of the Union because of the dead hand of Westminster politics which has become more colonised and controlled by forces of conservatism and neo-liberalism than elsewhere. Labour has shown no signs of making a significant and substantial break with 'new' Labour despite Miliband's leadership and Labour supports continued austerity measures. Moreover, despite a move to the left in the leadership of unions in the last decade, unions themselves remain too enfeebled to overcome these barriers and push for deep-seated social change either through the Labour Party or independently. Using an instrumental, cost/benefit analysis, suggests that by contrast, social change is relatively more possible under independence.

The Westminster roadblock

Since the late 1970s, the ideology of neo-liberalism – essentially, the market knows best and all human activities should be commodified for sale in the marketplace – has colonialized the political mainstream. The geographic centre of power in Britain is London and the centre of political power is Westminster. It is here that the neo-liberalism has applied itself so that it now dominates and is hegemonic. Despite the slight moderating influence of the devolution since 1999, the results are plain to see. Privatisation, marketization and commodification abound. The project of neo-liberalism has been about two things in particular – resolving the profitability crisis of capitalism by exploiting labour (workers) further, and by shifting power more fully back to towards capital (employers). Consequently, social inequality - measured by wealth and resources as well as life opportunities – has widened more than ever in the post-war period. Put more simply, we know live in an era of the super-rich and the working poor, of the plutocrats and the dispossessed. Despite the crisis of neo-liberalism and the attendant recession and austerity, the hold of neo-liberalism on the body politic is no less firm than it was before. This is a massive condemnation of the left, and especially of the far left in Britain which is headquartered in, and directed from, London. To use the nomenclature 'Westminster' and 'London' is not to engage in petty parochialism but merely to observe that the key political arena is found in the capital of Britain.

The hold of neo-liberalism has been buttressed and extended by the defeat of the key unions in the 1980s – the miners being the most important case - and by the collapse of the Soviet Union in 1990 as a form of 'actually existing socialism'. Both reinforced the objective and subjective sense that 'there is no alternative' (as Thatcher's TINA phrase meant) to the market. The result of these three factors – neo-liberalism itself, the defeat of the big battalions in the union movement, and the collapse of the Soviet Union – was 'new' Labour. The so-called 'third way' of Tony Blair, Gordon Brown and Peter Mandelson was a rejection of social democracy and an accommodation to neo-liberalism. Indeed, it was a variant of neo-liberalism called social liberalism, where the market could be harnessed to create (through economic growth) wealth that would trickle down and out of which some basic safety net could be provided for the weakest. The bargain between wealth creation and social provision was heavily tipped in favour of the economic side of the equation so that anything that got in the way of the market creating wealth was to be ended. The conditions for the economic growth to create the wealth demanded that capital was able to dictate them. It was for this reason that when Thatcher was asked in 2002 what her greatest achievement was, she replied: 'Tony Blair and New Labour. We forced our opponents to change their minds'.

Since that comment, the union movement has moved to the left judged by the rise of the 'awkward squad' of union leaders and in formal terms, at least, Labour is no longer 'new' Labour as Ed Miliband repudiated it after he became leader in September 2010. But this does not mean that Labour is any more left wing, radical or progressive because of these developments. Indeed, Labour in government was part and parcel of implementing not just neo-liberalism but also creating the economic crisis which we still endure. What is even starker is that despite the repudiation of 'new' Labour by Miliband, Labour under him has signally failed to ride the crest of the wave of popular discontent against neo-liberalism by offering a coherent alternative to it based upon restricting the operation of the market and moderating its outcomes. To that extent that Miliband and Labour are popular, it is mostly because they are not the government and are neither the Tories or Liberal Democrats. Miliband's espousal of 'responsible capitalism', 'pre-distribution' and then 'one nation-ism' are timid and simply not up to the task of solving, let alone ameliorating, the pressing social and economic inequalities and injustices that exist in our society. This has not been changed by his address to the 2013 Labour conference. It is a measure of how low ambitions have become that his address was so widely and positively received by the affiliated unions. For example, those that welcomed his proposed cap on energy prices rises seemed to have forgotten that put public utilities (including energy) into public ownership is really what is necessary.

For those on the left that are against independence, the capture of Unite, the biggest union and biggest union affiliate to Labour, by a radical left is seen to be a key game changer. Their argument is that Unite can and will drag the union movement and Labour to the left. This is far from a daft argument (even though the second and third biggest unions, Unison and the GMB respectively, do not appear to be particularly moved by this development). So this strategy is worthy of serious consideration.

Regulating capital

In arguing against independence, Richard Leonard (Morning Star 19 April 2013) has suggested that socialism is independence – independence from capitalism. On this point, he is right and this should be recognised. But his preferred route of the British-wide 'reclaim Labour project' is not convincing. Unlike many others on the left, his primary reason for articulating his case is that the ownership of the means of production, distribution and exchange in Scotland is based out Scotland. This is true. But given that ownership of the economy and the locus of its control is increasingly outside the geographical boundaries of the British Isles, it is not convincing to say that a British state – under instruction from the left - could do any more or less than a Scottish state – under instruction from the left - in regulating capital. Sure, there are certain things that can be done by either a Scottish or British state but, that said, the pressing need is to create trans-state and trans-national forms of regulation of capital through the international union movement, international law and global institutions. The salience of this is indicated by recognition that many of the largest employers are listed on the London Stock Exchange and headquartered in the City. So London is their geographical locus. But what pressures they respond to, and how they choose to act, are very much the result of global forces of which London is just one part.

Reclaiming Labour

The premise that a) Labour needs to become more radical in order to not only offer a genuine alternative to the Tories and Liberals but also b) give citizens the confidence that radical social change is not only desirable but possible, is a valid one. It is the basis that the current reclaim Labour project has been grounded upon since the early 2000s (and, of course, well before too). At various points in the run up to the 2005 and 2010 general elections, the unions affiliated to Labour seemed to be working together to change Labour Party policy. The signs of this were the Warwick I and Warwick II agreements, essentially the manifestos that Labour would fight the elections on. The main protagonists in forcing this change were the big unions of the GMB, Unite (formerly Amicus and the T&G) and Unison. The first point to note is that Warwick I and Warwick II were not exactly what the unions – who varied in their degrees of radicalism with Unison less radical than Unite – wanted. The unions made significant compromises on their agendas despite providing the lion's share of funding to Labour. The second point to note is that little of the substance of the Warwick I and Warwick II was actually used as the basis of the election campaigns by Labour. But these pale into insignificance when one recognises that election manifestos have never in recent times in the case of Labour been implemented in full. Instead, policies are watered down, delayed and ditched, indicating that the real power within Labour lies in the Parliamentary Labour Party (i.e., the MPs) and amongst the party leadership. This point about the fruits of the reclaim Labour project is reinforced all the more by the election of Ed Miliband as a result of union support over his brother in 2010. He has since made clear Labour's alternative to the austerity programme of the coalition government is essentially fewer cuts and less quickly. It is far from one of reflation of the economy and redistribution of wealth. So he has attacked unions for striking against pension reform, and said that pay freezes will be maintained, spending limits will be enforced and cuts will not be reversed under a Labour government. His big ideas have been 'pre-distribution', 'responsible capitalism' and the 'one-nation'. None of these offers much in the way of change nor a challenge to the powerful, vested interests that ultimately influence and control society. Fundamentally, Miliband is not prepared to use the state to regulate capitalism. All he is prepared to do is plead with capital to change its ways. And yet, all this was quite predictable. A union like Unite choose to back Miliband and not even allow John McDonnell MP to get onto the ballot for the leadership election even though McDonnell supported every Unite policy and his policies were very similar to those of Unite.

So the effectiveness of the project to reclaim Labour is not on strong ground even though its strongest and most sustained attempt is being made, particularly at the instigation of Unite. Moreover, Unite, the union that is most pushing the reclaim project, has not been consistent in pursuing this project. Over Miliband, it has flipped from strong criticism in early 2012 over 'responsible capitalism' to adulation over 'one nation' in late 2012 and back to criticism over responses to austerity in early 2013, and then in the summer of 2013 praise for what both Labour MP, John McDonnell, and PCS union general secretary, Mark Serwotka, dubbed 'austerity lite'. Then Unite highly praised Miliband for his speeches to the 2013 annual gatherings of the TUC and Labour Party, showing that it was lowering its political expectations of him and vastly over-estimating the significance of Miliband's policy announcements, dubbing them as a break with 'new' Labour's 'neo-liberal dogmas' (*Guardian* 12 October 2013). Consistent and trenchant criticism is necessary (if not sufficient) to force Miliband and the Labour leadership to skip to the beat of genuinely progressive policies. And, what Unite does or does not do is not the whole picture for the other big players are Unison and the GMB. Neither has shown any sign of moving to the left, as Unite has, and there is little reason to doubt this will change in the near future. Unison is the key union of the two (Unison, GMB) because it is by far and away the major union in the public sector. If Unison does not move on an issue in the public sector, the issue is unlikely to get very far - no matter how hard the other two unions (Unite, GMB) try because even together they do not outnumber Unison.

Then there is the question of how the values of the reclaim Labour project are to be enforced in policy and practice terms (even assuming the criticisms remain consistent and trenchant). Unite – along with a small number of other unions like the GMB – is trying more than ever before to get its activists selected as prospective parliamentary candidates for Labour for the 2015 general election. This is welcome because the strategy recognises that the locus of power within Labour is the Parliamentary Labour Party (and not annual conference, the national executive or the national policy forums). It offers the prospect of union member MPs promoting and abiding by union policy much more than union-sponsored MPs have ever done. Unite has by far the largest parliamentary group of union sponsored MPs – with over one hundred and fifty of these – but unlike the RMT or PCS parliamentary groups (led by John McDonnell) it does not seem to be capable of acting as a coherent and powerful force. But what the 'reclaim Labour' strategy does not recognise is that the locus of power within the Parliamentary Labour Party is actually the Shadow Cabinet. Labour shadow cabinets and Labour leaders of the opposition – and then as cabinets and prime ministers – have consistently ignored the will of the Parliamentary Labour Party when it has steered to the left. There is no reason to believe that the present or future will be any different.

This serious doubt about the ability of Unite, the biggest union and biggest union affiliate to Labour, to make the desired progress is reinforced when one considers that the scale of its ambition is quite limited. Unite has only targeted 41 constituencies (albeit the safer Labour seats) to get its candidates or those it favours selected as prospective candidates. Given both the Tory and Blairite backlash against Unite for its attempt to secure the Falkirk West nomination for its candidate, one may be mistaken for believing that Unite was – as per Falkirk - seeking to take over all of the Labour Party. It was not and could not for 41 targets out of a current crop of 258 Labour MPs shows that its operation is on the margins. By mid-

June 2013, it had only been successful in a dozen of these targeted seats. The other side to Unite's strategy was to get its members to join Labour in order to thus influence candidate selection and the party more widely. In December 2011, it set a target of 5,000 Unite members joining Labour. But by December 2012, only 600 had done so. And, in 2011-2012 some 492,000 Unite members opted out of paying the political levy (out of about 1m that did) according to the *Guardian* (23 July 2013). This indicates, inter alia, that Unite members of a more oppositional consciousness are unlikely to see supporting or joining Labour – much less being active within it – as a particularly attractive prospect. (It may even show that Unite activists and officers are not particularly motivated to recruit to Labour.) Even if Unite members view Labour and its leadership as part of the problem, it is by no means an obvious conclusion to join it and try to achieve change from within. Being active in one's union, community campaigns and other pressure groups is more likely to be the direction they would go in (suggesting the prospects of building a left-wing alternative to Labour are just as hard as reclaiming Labour, and vice-versa).

But let's put all that aside for the moment and assume rather rashly that a simple majority of Labour MPs were union members as per the Unite-type of initiative outlined above. With that assumption in place, the strategy of reclaiming Labour still does not take into account a number of factors. The first of these is that May 2015 is still some way off so there's a fair bit of waiting to be done. The second is that Labour may not win if the current polls are anything to go by and this means that Unite needs to be equally if not more active in the others strands of its strategy – on the industrial front, with the PCS union and working with forces outside Labour in the guise of the People's Assembly against Austerity and the Coalition of Resistance in particular. The third is that other unions are not being as nearly proactive as Unite is so it is easier for hostile forces to single out Unite. But more important than any of these is that in ideological and structural terms neither Labour nor the parliamentary system are capable of creating, facilitating or allowing such radical change. Of course, there is the longstanding argument that Labour is not a socialist party and never has been – being a social democratic one instead – and that parliament as an institution is predicated on preventing radical social change that challenges the vested interests of the ruling class in society. Relevant though these arguments still are, what is being argued here is that since these arguments were first made many decades ago by the likes of Ralph Miliband (father of Ed and David), there have been further developments which have added additional layers to the ability of Labour and parliament to enforce conservatism. Mostly obviously with regard to Labour has been its managerialisation and centralisation as a result of the diminution of union and constituency influence in its processes, organisational culture and structures. In terms of parliament, it has been more thoroughly colonised by business interests to the extent that their influenced is now embedded within its very operation. Underlying both phenomena is that popular participation in and engagement with both Labour (members, activists) and parliament are so atrophied in quantitative terms as to constitute a qualitative change for the worse. Now, of course, the wider implications of these phenomena for the project of radical social change under independence cannot be discounted either but they are not so grave as they are for the reclaim Labour project.

And, to reinforce the point here, Ed Miliband is not just the expression of the problem but part of the edifice of the problem itself and as Labour is currently constituted. Unite was key to getting Ed elected as leader over his brother yet if Unite thought Ed was a political ally, it has been sorely mistaken. Unite has continually warned Miliband that he is in danger of losing working class support with his regressive, out-of-touch policies. It keeps advising him to change course. The problem with this approach is that Miliband is the problem and no amount of friendly advice will change this. Moreover, Miliband is not in danger of losing working class support with his policies – he has already lost much working class support because of these policies.

Conclusion

Because of the weakness of the left on a British-wide basis and its inability to change Labour from the inside or the outside, the result of voting to maintain the Union will be to maintain neo-liberalism and austerity. This is not what those on the left that vote 'no' desire and intend but it is, nevertheless, the practical end result. This conclusion is reinforced by the unwillingness of the Better Together campaign to promote a case for social justice by staying in the Union. This would require wealth redistribution which it will not countenance. But the conclusion is also reinforced by the direction of the Scottish Labour Party under Johann Lamont. Despite being the left wing candidate in the leadership election, she has maintained the rightward trajectory of Scottish Labour and its tribal stance towards anything remotely progressive that the SNP proposes. Lamont's questioning of universal benefits at a time when they are needed most by the vulnerable is an indication of succumbing to a neo-liberal agenda. The simple way to resolve the issue is not to introduce means testing but to make the well-off pay over the odds for their prescriptions and the like by instituting a system of progressive taxation where they pay considerably more and stop evading their income and corporate tax responsibilities.

Chapter 3: The possibility of radical social change under independence

Introduction

The argument presented in this book is that independence for Scotland as a new state gives not just greater latitude to change but also facilitates the inclination to take a certain direction towards social change. On the one hand, this is because the freedom of the institutions of the polity of an independent Scotland will be that much greater than under the Union (notwithstanding that there would not be total freedom – see chapter 7). On the other hand, this is because the tangible and longstanding social democratic impulse in Scottish society – the 'red thread' – has become reconfigured and reinforced since the 1980s battle against Thatcherism into a radical form of national identity and what it means to be 'Scottish' (see below). However, under devolution since 1999, this social democratic impulse has had a limited ability to gain representation in the body politic because of the maintenance of reserved business to Westminster, the dominance of politics by the Parliament and the conservatism of both Scottish Labour and the SNP. However, under independence, the SNP is likely to fragment around the edges as its central goal has been achieved, giving rise to a new left as the SNP's left wing joins forces with others. This will also drag the Scottish Labour Party to the left so that the centre of political gravity will be more firmly embedded on the social democratic left. Under this reconfiguration, the left will play a far larger role in shaping society in Scotland and will be able to make its mark under the greater institutional freedom of independence. This process will help mark the renewal of the radical left after the implosion of the once significant Scottish Socialist Party (SSP) in 2006 following the disastrous actions of Tommy Sheridan. But the ease and pace of this process should not be overstated because the SNP will not simply implode after independence. Instead, it is likely to become the institutionalised governing party and as such many will wish to stay in the party of power than take their chances on the emerging new left. To say that the SNP could mirror the ANC in South Africa is not too far from the truth in this regard because being in power is an attractive and comfortable place to be for politicians (existing and aspiring).

So this chapter talks in terms not of independence providing the (absolute) freedom for citizens in Scotland to make society take its own social democratic course but the greater latitude to do so. There is good reason to use this cautious and measured language (rather than talk in the normal lexicon of the left of overblown exaggeration and hyperbole). First, because Scotland will remain integrated into the capitalist world economy as no form of autarky is being contemplated. Second, because the nature of independence is up for grabs and cannot be regarded as already being known. The former means that external restrictions will exist and the latter means that some within the pro-independence forces will be more willing and able to succumb – if not actually agree – with what these external forces (like the International Monetary Fund (IMF), World Trade Organisation (WTO), World Bank, European Central Bank (ECB) etcetera) say. In other words, the forces of neo-liberalism as a particular form of capitalism will be present and the strength of these internal and external forces means that instituting radical social change will be no stroll in the park. But there is also the factor of the current weakness of the left to be added in. As a whole the left – inside and outside Labour - is weaker than it once was throughout Britain. Developments in the SSP have made this situation much worse. Against this has to be held some small signs of renewal around the Radical Independence Campaign and of the SSP itself. Nonetheless, the left's ability to influence political developments is sufficiently poor as to mean this cannot be glossed over.

Gaining traction for radical independence

We need to start off with some home truths in order to get the right kind of perspective on how to gain traction for a radical vision of independence. First, Scotland is not an oppressed nation so any 'national question' cannot and will not be on a par with those national struggles for liberation elsewhere in the word. Second, it is more difficult to campaign for – than against – something because it takes greater resources and initiative, and the left has become (almost necessarily) habituated into campaigning against things as a result of the political initiative lying with neo-liberalism. Third, and even though the 'no' campaign has not been able to argue a positive case for the Union, its advantage is that it will win by default as it is the status quo. There is a fear and uncertainty amongst many of what independence could bring about and the 'no' campaign is very adept at tapping into this with cataclysmic pronouncements so that this group of voters feels out of its comfort zone. Ironically, the 'no' argument is aided by the SNP's tactic of presenting its version of independence as a form of federalist 'devo-max' (see Chapter 5) because the two (independence, federalist 'devo-max') seem so contradictory.

Given this, in the following, a key argument of the book – maybe the key argument of this book - is expounded. This is that in convincing voters to cast their preference for independence on 18 September 2014, the left must make the argument that independence merely provides the opportunity to create radical social change. 2014 is but just one third of the equation – the other thirds are the 2016 Scottish Parliament elections and the mobilisation of social forces outside the parliamentary system in order to exert influence on legislature, executive, judiciary and so on. But more than that, the argument here is that the way to successfully tackle the three targets – 2014, 2016, extra-parliamentary activity – is to concentrate upon the material (social, economic) issues that make a strong connection with the mass of citizens. These are their deprivations in terms of living standards for them, their families and their communities – their housing, employment, education, benefits, transport and health and so on. The end point of the argument the left makes is that we must convince these people that their lives will be significantly better off under independence. Let's put a figure on this – of say £5,000 per annum. This is not money they will have in their bank accounts each year of independence but the value of what they will gain in a number of areas of their lives – housing, employment, health, education etc. In other words, we need to be able to quantify what the benefits of a radical version of independence will look like. Otherwise, we will remain in the realm of flights of fantasy. But if all this was we had to do it would be relatively easy. Of course, it is not.

Before moving on to that, it is worth pointing out that the figure of £5,000 pa has not been plucked out of thin air. Rather, the opposite is true. In two opinion polls from the Scottish Social Attitudes Survey of December 2011 and September 2013, support for independence doubled its levels from a third to two thirds if those polled believed that they would be £500pa better off under independence. This indicates that the connection of living standards and income to the case for independence is not only a positive one but a critical one too. However, £500pa is an insufficiently ambitious increase and would not make a significant difference to those living standards and the extent of social inequality so the figure of £5,000pa was selected. The point of departure for Salmond, the SNP and Yes Scotland has been to fly in the face of this by continually stressing that independence is about achieving the goal of national self-determination and decisions affecting Scotland made by people in Scotland. This heftily places the means before the ends. But more than that – and as explained later on – national self-determination does not guarantee social justice for independence could take different forms such as capitalist independence or social democratic independence. Eventually, when Salmond gets to the point of talking about material concerns – fairness and prosperity, in his words – this is expressed in such vacuous, unspecific terms as to be pretty meaningless and unattractive[1].

Returning to the issue of the other pressing tasks for the campaigners for radical independence, the challenge of presenting a credible and compelling case for radical independence that becomes ultimately convincing can only come about when the argument above is made to people in the context of collective campaigns which articulate their material grievances. The anti-bedroom tax campaign is one such example. By making the argument to them in this way and in these arenas, a strong connection can be made about their current situation and their future prospects. If these arguments are just presented as a leaflet through a letter box, an email, a phonecall, a text etc without being embedded in the context of collective campaigns which articulate their material grievances, our arguments will come across as well-meaning but fanciful to say the least. The difference is that people will be able to see – as a result of the collective campaigns – that there is a way in which their grievances can be resolved in their favour because the social forces that they represent can exert leverage upon the vested interests of our current political system[2]. These requisite social forces are the actions and organisations of the very people who have the grievances. This is the lesson of the poll tax revolt in both Scotland and England.

If it was not apparent already, let's make this abundantly clear – the majority of citizens can only and will only be moved to vote and push for a radical form of independence based upon the furtherance of their material interests. The issues of campaigning to remove Trident and end imperialism, war and racism and the like are not the prime movers for this. They can at best play a secondary, supporting role where they - along with the institution of progressive taxation - provide the necessary finance to fund better social provision because they money that is spent on Trident and fighting foreign wars is spent elsewhere. It's a case of hospital beds not nuclear bombs and welfare not warfare – but with the proviso that we do not use that as the starting point for our pitch to them.

How traction can come about for radical independence and what it looks like

This multi-component argument will now be laid out in greater detail and worked through logically on a step-by-basis. So before getting caught up in the potential passion and intensity of outlining what a socially progressive Scotland could look like (see next chapter), the left needs to outline a convincing case of exactly how this radical form and content of independence can come about. The passion of the case for getting rid of Trident nuclear weapons or stopping the 'bedroom tax', for example, is often matched by the passion by which the case is made for getting rid of Trident nuclear weapons or stopping the 'bedroom tax'. To draw upon the formula used earlier, this passion is necessary but not sufficient to get traction for the case for (radical) independence. Inspiration and exhortation have a role to play but only a role. Indeed, the argument of the anti-independence forces on such matters is worthy of examination because it should not be assumed that support for radical social change necessarily leads to support for independence nor that the logic of getting rid of Trident nuclear weapons or stopping the 'bedroom tax' dictates that independence is the only modus operandi. A dispassionate analysis would analyse what the balance of social forces and their dynamics are so as to work out the best course of action. This is an instrumental not ideological matter – a matter of strategy and resources, not principles and dogma. Therefore, the concrete links have to be made in a chain of causation so that it can be demonstrated that getting from A (the present) to Z (the desired future) does require independence. Too often the links are never explained or even made explicit. Too often it is a matter of faith and not logic.

In addition to this, the specificity of the goal and purpose of radical independence has to be taken into account. In any campaign or social movement, there are fairly definite aims and objectives and these are relatively narrow and low level, especially when concerned with the removal or ending of 'x' or 'y' as per the anti-poll tax revolt, the anti-war movement or the anti-apartheid campaign. Of course, within these milieus there were strands and strains for this and that so there were positive cases for alternatives. But the widest, deepest and strongest unity and sense of purpose pertained to being against the poll tax etcetera and wanting their removal and ending. When applied to the campaign for independence, the task of persuasion is more difficult because it is a campaign for something and that something is very broad and large, being a new type of society. While emanating from being against certain things like Trident, war, poverty and the like, this worldview as a whole worldview is not organically and intimately connected to the economic and social experiences of the mass of citizens and their attendant grievances and deprivations. Indeed, it is several stages removed from these precisely because the radical view of independence is to imagine a new type of society on an abstracted basis. This makes the task of campaigning for independence that much more difficult. Put another way round, the campaign for independence does not spring organically from the struggle of workers for higher wages, more secure jobs or of citizens for better education and health for their children. It is the task for campaigners for independence to explore and identify the links so that they can make the connections more concrete. Those on the left against independence may think this lack of organic connection proves their point about the need to maintain the Union (albeit of a different type). It does not – for the case for the Union is equally unconnected with the well-spring of economic and social experiences of the mass of citizens and their attendant grievances and deprivations. Class is certainly the fault line here but it does not necessarily determine in and of itself the practical, spatial dimensions on which the battle is fought – be they local, regional, national, inter- or trans-national. Consequently, this is a voyage of exploration that must be made and made quickly if the radical left is to find the necessary connections.

But as if this was not enough, then there is a final problematic to be considered (and resolved). Notwithstanding the valiant efforts of the Radical Independence Campaign (RIC) and those that attended the independence demonstrations of September 2012 and September 2013, there is no independence movement, no movement for independence at presence (and nor is one likely to emerge anytime soon or at all). For there to be a social movement for independence requires that certain quantitative and qualitative conditions are met. If you think of the union movement, the women's movement, the anti-racist movement and so on in their heydays, it was easy to see what was manifest about them – namely, coherence of organisation, purpose and values (no matter the heterogeneity and diversity). There is no such coherence of organisation, purpose and values to the campaign for independence[3]. Indeed, the campaign for independence is precisely that – a campaign and not a (social) movement because – and in line with what was argued immediately above – it does not spring organically from citizens' collective grievances. Nor does it have the social weight and ballast needed to be a movement. This is what is meant by the quantitative (i.e., breadth) and qualitative (i.e., depth) conditions. Again, none of this means the case for the status quo (of whatever hue) is any more correct or grounded. The Better Together campaign is even less of a campaign than Yes Scotland is. But that should be of little consolation as the independence campaign faces a bigger challenge to secure its objective that do the anti-independence forces to secure theirs.

This, hopefully, brings the question foursquare back to the pressing issue of just how does the radical campaign for independence gain traction for its ideas and policies with the clock marching inwards to 18 September 2014. There are two – necessarily connected – ways to do this. Identifying the suitable collective grievances that provide not only the basis for generalisation to - and across - wide strata of citizens but also collective mobilisation is the first critical task. Radical independence activists must become involved and respected within these milieus (and the milieu must be substantial enough to have social weight). Only with that is there the prospect of raising the case for independence in a serious way. But it must be done with finesse so that the second task can be achieved. Thus, independence is not the immediate answer to social questions, especially as it will not change society quickly (see before) and struggles can and should be won in the here and now. But for those wishing to see significant structural change in society in terms of its distribution of wealth, resources and power or those wishing to see the removal of much of the basis to the situations that continuously give rise to the struggles they are involved in, then the case for radical independence can be a serious attraction. It is in this measured way that the links between the present and the future can be forged.

Now, of course, if the collective grievances and mobilisations do not emerge in the required number and intensity prior to September 2014 like an anti-poll tax revolt then the attempt to link them to the case for radical independence is likely to be stillborn. Take the example of the campaign against Trident as an example. It is the interest of an active minority in terms of those that are part of the mobilisations at Faslane and the like. They are supported by a large number of passive layers. Yet the issue has not gained mass traction despite the attempt to turn 'swords into ploughshares' and slogans like '(hospital) beds not bombs'. So what might be some suitable alternatives? The bedroom tax seems an obvious one but sizeable though the protests have been (especially in Glasgow compared to the rest of Britain) and notable the success against evictions achieved, this is not an issue which can become the new poll tax, much less the issue that can become the midwife of independence. This is because the numbers directly and materially affected are relatively small and because, unlike the poll tax, there is not the same ability not to pay. Unfortunately, it does not seem to be likely that the existing struggles against job losses (especially in the public sector), the reform of public sector pensions or the continuation of pay freezes in the public sector provide much of an alternative either. The fight against job losses has never really got off the ground, the pensions fight has been winding down since the mass strike of 30 November 2011 and only the PCS union has made a fist of fighting the government pay freeze. This does leave the campaign for radical independence with a considerable problem because even if it recognises the necessity of gaining traction in this way, the aforementioned campaigns and issues will be far from sufficient to do the job required. There is always the possibility that new issues might emerge, that a particular issue might become a lightning rod for opposition to the Coalition government and so bring to the surface active discontent on other issues. But there are no guarantees.

The Red Thread

Compared to the population of England, the citizens of Scotland have consistently displayed more progressive attitudes and values across a range of social, economic and political issues over the last three decades. This is not to make out that all is well in Scotland – despite there being more pandas than Tory MPs in Scotland – because when the detail is delved into, recent Scottish Social Attitudes have shown the gap is narrowing and overall neo-liberalism is reducing the extent of progressive attitudes of those on both sides of the border. Moreover, we are essentially talking of the urban areas and especially the central belt and not the whole of Scotland as the location of these progressive persuasions. And, the attitudes and values displayed in this geographic entity then do not seem quite so radical and progressive when compared to those similarly urbanised areas of north-west England, north-east England and south Wales. But none of those regions – with the exception of south Wales – have the added ingredient of a national sense of consciousness, a national identity – by which to express and articulate these attitudes and values. The consequence is that despite the central belt far from constituting the whole of Scotland, in fact, it does overwhelmingly define what it means to be 'Scottish' and what the aspirations of the majority of citizens are. Traditionally, the Labour Party – and to a small degree the Communist Party, Scottish Militant Labour and the SSP too – embodied these values and aspirations. The argument here is not that national identity is in any way the salvation of a radical vote for independence. Far from it but it is to acknowledge the forms of social capital and institutions in which it is expressed like higher union membership, higher degrees of council house provision and a 'municipal socialism' form of local government.

Let's put the issue the other way around. If the actively-induced path to independence (outlined above and the essence of this book) cannot be assured then is there some possibility of salvation from the passively-induced path (of relying on the more progressive social attitudes)? It should not be ruled out but it is a bit like the risky last throw of the dice in a high stakes game of poker. Yes, there is a strong social democratic impulse which is latent in society in Scotland but it is far a more persuasive and pervasive force when it is active through connection to collective, progressive struggles (rather than just evidenced in survey, opinion polls and elections). When the social democratic impulse is most vibrant and manifest, a supply and demand process takes place. It emerges out of struggles and transfers its presence into culture and politics which then reinforces the possibility of other such struggles. In other words, the social democratic impulse is not free standing, existing in a vacuum. So if the latent red thread is to play a key role, it is more likely to do so when connected and brought to life by active struggles, where it provides a foundation to these struggles.

With that in mind, it is worth itemising the red thread in society in Scotland. To repeat again, the argument is not that Scots are innately or inherently more radical than their Welsh or English counterparts. Certainly, the same degrees of radicalism on issues of wealth distribution (taxation and expenditure), who society is for (protection of the weak and vulnerable), class relations ('them and us', 'have and have nots'), power ('one law for them and another for us') and tolerance of difference and diversity (gender, sexuality, race, religion etc) can be found in other parts of Britain and specifically in parts of England (like the north-west or north-east). But Scotland and Wales are usually more radical than the most radical regions of England. And the construction of these views - like any others - is the outcome of collective political struggles, past and present. Rather, the argument is that the emergence of a national identity which continues to be social democratic in orientation as a result of the popular revolt against Thatcher and Thatcherism is a far more potent political force than any regional identity which became infused with the politics of anti-Thatcherism (as those of the north-west or north-east England did). The potency of this political force in Scotland has been reinforced by the existence of a definable sense of there being a distinct Scottish political process (especially after the creation of the Parliament in 1999) which has existed alongside the British, European and international political processes. The British and Scottish social attitudes surveys highlight this in two ways. First, that more (objectively) middle class people in Scotland still self-identify themselves as (subjectively) working class. Second, more Scots self-identify as 'Scottish' rather than 'British' than English do as 'English' rather than 'British'. When these come together, these provide the basis that what is means to be 'Scottish' is predominantly defined in a progressive way, hence, the use of the term the 'red thread'. But is also true that these political and social values have not recently and do currently not find much of a home in the either the SNP or the Scottish Labour Party. There are many in both parties that do aspire for their particular parties to articulate these but that does not change the matter of what the parties are in reality. Similarly, the implosion of the SSP does not change the fact that it is no longer able to articulate these values in a way that it once did, namely, as a sizeable and credible political party.

Conclusion

The 'Better Together' vote 'no' campaign does not have a positive message for the case for the Union. Its message is predicated on fear and fear of change. It is a camp rather than a campaign as it is internally split given that Labour will not work with the Tories and has set up its own campaign called 'United with Labour'. But it too suffers from the same defects of a singularly negative message. Neither 'Better Together' nor 'United with Labour' show any inclination, for example to adopt the perspective of the Common Weal. Despite promises of enhanced devolution, both are forced into defending the status quo. All this provides some advantage to the argument for a radical form of independence. So too does the 'red thread' where the expression 'We're all Jock Tamson's bairns' sums up the common belief that those ordinary citizens living in Scotland (and which are outside membership of the elites in society) all exist under the same yoke while also articulating the aspirations of egalitarianism and equality by these people.

But though these are useful phenomena to be mindful of, they do not detract from the fundamentals that gaining traction for the case for a radical form of independence means that material grievances must become the means of traction as this chapter has argued. This means that active, collective mobilising campaigns on these grievances. And, it will not be enough to merely vote for a radical form of independence not only because it is not on the ballot paper but because if independence is won the SNP will try to shape it in a moderate, conservative way. Fighting for change in 2014 must also mean fighting for change in 2016 and in the extra-parliamentary arenas of society. To envisage such a situation is to see that from anger can spring the hope of positive change and which then produces collective action (hence the trinity of anger > hope > action that social movements speak of).

Chapter 4 What Scotland could be like

Introduction

The whole rationale for seeking independence is to gain the levers of power to achieve far greater economic and social justice than we have - and can have - under the current political set-up. It is about the possibility of then developing a socialised economy as part of a socialised, democratic and civilised society. Some call this a mixed economy, some call it social democracy and others still socialism. For the time being, we do not have to get too hung up on the terminology (although it is worth bearing in mind that social democracy – where the market exists but is regulated – is not the same was socialism which is broadly defined as a society run by workers for workers). This makes it clear that social democracy is about re-ordering what society and economy look like, the bases upon which they operate and the outcomes they give rise to. Collectively, this would mean that the regulation of the market would moderate its outcomes of inequality in a way that would see human need come before private profit. This helps outline what independence is for and as well as what independence is from. Such ideas have recently been promoted by the Jimmy Reid Foundation through its Commonweal project.

Scotland is a sufficiently wealthy entity that we do not have to be concerned with whether it is economically feasible that Scotland could become an independent state and country. The issue to be tackled is to how to go about redistributing this wealth from the rich to the poor and how to ensure a far more equitable ownership and control of - as well as benefit from - the resources that reside within Scotland (i.e., forms of human, financial, technological, physical etc capital). In other words, the future of a radical, progressive Scotland is not dependent upon economic growth (as the SNP maintains). To repeat again, this does not mean that Scotland would become 'Cuba with midgies' as the right used to describe the aspiration of a socialist Scotland. In fact, Scotland could become far more like the small economies of Scandinavia (notwithstanding that their social progress has been eroded in recent years by internal and external political changes).

Ending market madness

The capitalist (free) market has increasingly dominated our lives as privatisation and marketization of the public sector and services have taken grip. But the market now operates in areas of our lives that are new and disturbing as a result of the commodification for profit of leisure, and care of children, the infirm and elderly. The case for radical independence is about stating that a) there are areas of society where the operation of the market is not appropriate, and b) there is a need to regulate the processes and outcomes of the market where it does still operate. The corollary to this is that non-market mechanisms for replacing the market are not predicated on re-introducing renationalisation as it was experienced in the post-war period but as a new democratic form of public ownership which is not necessarily state-based and is premised upon popular participation and control. These forms of social ownership would not just enhance social equality but also enhance the level of democracy and the degree of citizen participation as elite groups would be disenfranchised of their power to determine how our lives are run. These forms of social ownership could occur through cooperatives and mutuals as much as they might through state ownership. But if the latter form was to be used, the practice and experience would need to be wholly different from the experience of the national industries which were run and controlled by a mixture of civil servants and politicians or other public organisations like NHS trusts which are increasingly dominated by professional elites.

So a radical version of independence would see the market taken out of operation in certain areas of society – childcare, education, health and so on being the most obvious candidates. But it would also make sense to remove the market from the natural monopolies like the railways, bus transport and the utilities (gas, electricity, telecommunications) because they are of such strategic importance to the operation of a decent and civilised society. Moreover, in terms of moving from coal, gas and oil-fired energy generation and towards wave, wind and tidal energy generation, the state is best oversee this through state ownership and control (given the huge capital resources required). When it turns to other areas of the economy and society, the regulation of the processes and outcomes of the operation of the market could include price caps on rent in the private sector, control of prices on basic commodities like food and children's clothing and limits on company profits where public sector work is undertaken. This would be the sense in which the state and the law could regulate the processes and outcomes of the market, ending fuel poverty, child poverty, the working poor and so on. But these are not the only ways. The most obvious other one is to provide legal and public policy support for unions so that they become capable of effectively defending their members' interests. This would mean a number of things such as repealing the anti-union laws of the 1980s which prevent workers being able to organise solidarity action to support each other. But it would also include compelling employers to negotiate with unions – and on sectoral basis so that employers cannot play 'divide and rule' and so that unions can aggregate their influence. Sectoral bargaining would also take wages out of competition between the different employers in the sector, ending the drive to compete on labour costs. Finally, a system of co-determination as in Germany could be instituted whereby statutory works councils exist at the workplace level and workers sit on the boards of companies and organisations as worker directors.

But much more can be done. Take the issue of wages and wage policy. Already there is a growing willingness in some parts of the public sector (like local government) to pay the 'living wage'. This could be extended to the private sector - and without giving tax breaks for employers to do so for this is essentially taxpayers paying for the higher wages and not the employers. But much more could be done, such as implementing a 'maximum wage' so that the ratio of the highest to lowest paid is brought down from 1:400 to something like 1:20. Another idea would be the 'solidarity wage' where the structure and inequity of wages remains unchanged at the point of payment but the taxation system is then used to redistribute from the rich to the poor. Such ideas would become less subject to derision and ridicule under an independent, radical Scotland and more likely to gain popular traction, raising the possibility of them becoming an actuality.

The same is true for how to deal with two of the major pressing problems faced currently, namely, economic stagnation, and the continuation of the banking crisis. The standard response from the left is quite rightly to oppose austerity (in almost all its guises except nuclear weapons and spending on the armed forces) and to advocate higher public spending in order to reflate the economy by stimulating growth. What is missing from this strategy is the recognition that to reflate under a neo-liberal framework will result in a) the rich disproportionately benefitting from the fruits of economic growth; b) the recurrence of the boom and slump cycle of capitalism because its dynamics remain unaltered; and c) further degradation of the environment. So reflation is necessary but its fruits not only must be redistributed but the basis upon which reflation takes place must be different, including the use of cooperatives and mutuals. Moreover, the basis on which the economic is structured requires fundamental change not just in terms of public ownership but also the move to a higher wage economy so that income levels can be raised and so that tax revenues can be increased (to pay for the social wage and to end the effective subsidisation of low pay).

Intimately connected to the continuation of economic stagnation is the position of the banks. Incredibly, and despite their major part in bring about the economic recession and stagnation through the 'credit crunch' and 'bad lending', they remain still subject to 'light touch' regulation. Why is this? Essentially, it is because they have been allowed to become too big – too big to be allowed to fail and too big to be told what to do and how to do it by anyone else. And equally incredibly despite the amount of taxpayers' money propping them up, the government is more dependent upon the banks than the banks are dependent upon the government. Again, too big to be told what to do and how to do it. Radical restructuring is needed but much more than this is also needed. Separating the high street, consumer operations from the investment operations would help but not that much. A much more effective way would be to a) compel the high street, consumer operations to become mutuals like the building societies and credit cooperatives are; and b) to enforce tight regulation upon the investment operations so not only are they not risky but they are also not unethical (in terms of the investing in companies and regimes that degrade the environment, stifle democracy and turn a blind eye to corruption).

If a future Scottish economy was primarily based upon attracting foreign investment, then it would necessarily compete on wages, conditions and government grants with other national economies. No mattered how educated, skilled and committed workers are in Scotland, they will be in competition with workers elsewhere. If, however, the economy in Scotland had at its centre a large sector of cooperatives, mutuals and other forms of socialised ownership, then there would not be the same self-induced pressure to compete on wages and the like. Such a type of economy does exist in the Basque country in Spain. The Mondragon organisation of cooperatives is the seventh largest economic player in the Spanish economy and has evaded recession unlike the rest of Spain (and elsewhere). It is not comprised of wholefood producers and retailers (like Suma, Britain's biggest worker cooperative) but of manufacturing, construction, retail, training and finance cooperatives that provide part of an interlocking and self-sustaining community. Mondragon is not an autarky of closed off, backward looking organisations and is far from perfect. It has significant wage differentials between workers and managers and is rather more worker-owned than worker-managed. It could benefit from rotating tasks and job enlargement so that workers play a far more significant management role. Nonetheless, it does show that an advanced economy can be run on socialised and democratised lines.

Participatory democracy

The rise of neo-liberalism has led to a closing off of certain questions and issues in society. Foremost amongst these is the participation of citizens in the running and determining of their own lives. Traditionally, the model has been of representative, indirect democracy whereby citizens vote every few years in elections for political parties to represent their interests. Here, civil society organisations attempted to influence the agenda that parties adopted both in and out of office. The rise of neo-liberalism has had two discernible effects. First, to limit the effective range of choice that voters have because all mainstream parties have been colonised by a neo-liberal agenda. Thus, a form of managerialism has taken over by which the only agenda is managing to affect growth of the economy without regard to issues of wealth re-distribution, existing power structures or degradation of the environment. Second, to constrain how political parties in office operate in terms of believing not only that market solutions are best but that there are only market solutions and that the advocates of the market – like management – know best how to undertake and implement these solutions. The outcome here is that more and more areas of society are now not subject to any control or scrutiny by the organs of representative democracy.

The effect of both is to reduce the popular participation – now called engagement - even further. Citizens do not see the point as all parties are pretty much the same, nothing changes no matter who is in office and professional elites have taken over the running of society. Of course, this could occasion the opposite response that power needs to be taken back from the elites and that people need to 'empower' themselves. But so far, it has not taken this path. The role, therefore, of a radically reconstituted society in Scotland under independence would be to not only encourage participatory, direct democracy but to embed the very processes and institutions by which it can occur within the fabric of the economy and society. This would necessarily mean more than just ensuring there are representatives of the majority of 'ordinary' citizens like workers in existing institutions like parliament and local authorities. It would necessarily mean creating new institutions to cover new areas of society (especially for those like economic and industrial democracy). The experience of Mondragon maybe one model that is followed by there are others like Michael Albert's Parecon (participatory economy) idea. Indeed, it raises the issue of the devolution of power and authority within Scotland so that Edinburgh and Holyrood do not become the new London and Westminster of old.

Conclusion

We are often led to believe we live in a meritocracy (now updated as 'strivers not scroungers'). The ability of citizens to believe that has become ever more tarnished as Labour under Blair became enthralled to the markets and their money(ed) men. Now the Conservatives have taken the 'one law for us (the rich), one for you (the poor)' a stage further with a cabinet dominated by millionaires and a government working at the behest of business to further privatise the public services and further deregulate the operation of the market. But let's not kid ourselves that prior to Blair and Cameron that all was much rosier in the garden. Even when it could be said that equality of opportunity existed – with substantial upward social mobility for many working class families up until the mid-1970s – it was still the case that most were left in the social class of fewer life opportunities, whether judged by health (physical, mental), wealth, education, housing, employment and the like. Equality of opportunity has never meant equality of decent outcome for the majority. Indeed, it has only meant equality of outcome where a large swathe of citizens is left with the same situation of poor housing, poor health, poor education, poor jobs and the like. A vision of how Scotland could be – under a radical form of independence – could see huge strides made towards equality of outcome at a decent level. Terms such as the 'working poor' and 'benefit scroungers' would fade away into disuse as work would be made to pay properly and workers would not be forced into unemployment and under-employment. What this type of society is called by many would range from anything from social democracy to socialism. At this point in time, such labels are not too important – rather, what society achieves for the majority of its citizens is.

Chapter 5 Why the SNP cannot be relied upon

Introduction

The SNP long ago ceased to be 'Tartan Tories', dominated by the farming and fishing communities of the Borders and the north-east of Scotland. While there are still a considerable number of such old nationalists within the SNP as well as thoroughly new neo-liberals, it has in the main become a modern, European left-of-centre party. Much of this positive reputation comes about as the Tories moved right - away from the kind of softer 'one nation' politics of one time leader, Edward Heath. Put more bluntly, Thatcher helped give the SNP a huge makeover in this department. But most of this reputation comes from the more recent phenomenon of Blair transforming the Labour Party from one that was notionally a social democratic party to one that was a variant of neo-liberalism (called social liberalism). And, of course, 'new' Labour also supported and continued with a foreign policy and defence strategy that was thoroughly unethical and imperialist. Yet despite the image and the reality of the SNP as left-of-centre, its neoliberal economics policy still heavily outweighs and critically undermines its more leftward stances on social issues, and social justice per se. This means that it is not a social democratic party and that it is not especially left wing. It just looks better than what is on offer from the other mainstream parties. To use the turn of phrase, in the kingdom of the blind, the one-eye man is king. Or if the SNP was likened to old right wing Labour MP, Roy Hattersley, he began to look radical from the late 1990s onwards simply because he stayed the same while others (like Kinnock, Brown and Darling) galloped past him to the right.

This chapter is not about saying the SNP cannot be trusted because they are nationalists, bourgeois or otherwise. But it is about saying that radicals and socialists cannot – consciously or otherwise – think the SNP can be relied upon or even cajoled into adopting that radical policies that are needed to attain a radical version of independence. This is the case whether the SNP is led by Alex Salmond or Nicola Sturgeon. The required trajectory towards radicalism in Scotland will come from other political parties and social forces. Indeed, the SNP's time in government since 2007 has been about trying to be all things to almost all people, and this inevitably means compromises which leave the poorer and weaker in a worse position. The SNP has been about showing it is fair but not (too) challenging. Take the example of its council tax freeze. It has been projected as a way to stop low income families from paying more. But the sharper observation is to see that while there is some partial truth to this, it is far from the whole picture. The freeze is a flat rate freeze on a regressive form of taxation so the wealthier benefit most, revenue for providing services for the most needy is effectively capped and it is also perfectly possible to freeze the banding rates for lower incomes while increasing it for higher incomes in order to generate more income for services.

The politics of the SNP

In contradistinction to Westminster governments, the SNP Scottish governments have refused to introduce tuition fees for Scottish students entering higher education, cancelled all PFI and PPP contracts within the NHS in Scotland (introduced by Labour), maintained free personal care for the elderly as well as free bus passes for the elderly (both also introduced by Labour) and introduced free prescriptions. None of these are to be sniffed at but closer examination reveals not everything is quite what it seems. The no tuition fees policy is being funded by the introduction of swingeing cuts to the funding of FE colleges, a traditional route onto university for students from low income backgrounds. The SNP's Scottish Future Trust, begun in 2008, is not the antithesis of PFI and PPP for it still uses private finance to invest in infrastructure projects, NHS included. When it comes to international issues, opposition to the war in Iraq was not all it seemed for the SNP pledged to end Scotland's participation in 'illegal wars'. So, if the United Nations sanctioned a western-dominated invasion of a country the SNP would presumably support it because it was 'legal'. And, the SNP supported the war in Afghanistan and the NATO intervention in Libya. On occasions, the SNP holds Norway up as a model for independent Scotland. Significantly, Norway is not an EU member and has created a hugely successful oil fund for future generations by having a nationalised oil industry. Yet, the SNP is too conservative to either nationalise the oil industry (or even heavily regulate it) nor contemplate the greater freedom that being outside the EU would give[4].

Behind the formal politics of the SNP lies another import facet of its practical politics. This is that it is a highly centralised and managerial operation, run by a professional elite of party workers and elected politicians. The sense in which it is a highly democratic and participative organisation comprising different and contending interest groups is absent (although this, of course, does not make it different from most other mainstream political parties). Consequently, and especially under Salmond's leadership, the SNP has no competition or counter-balance to the party hierarchy. Branches, national councils and party conferences are not the locus of power in the SNP. Instead, the party hierarchy is very much the permanent and full-time personnel of the party leadership. Thus, it is not often that the full weight of the party bureaucracy and leadership authority has to be used to get its own way – but when it is used (as was the case over the debate on membership of NATO in the October 2012 party conference), it is extremely powerful. Therefore, even if the SNP was to adopt more left-wing policies (such as those espoused by the Jimmy Reid Foundation), there is no guarantee that these would be implemented by an SNP government in an independent Scotland. For example, conference policies could be ignored and policies changed or watered down while in government as a result of perceived need by the leadership. In other words, it would only take events after a policy was adopted to bring about the reneging of that policy because it was deemed to clash with some perceived new 'reality'. Such an occasion might be what the capital markets think about this or that, or the emergence of another recession.

Tartan neo-liberalism

Despite what it professes when it talks about social compassion and decency, when the SNP is scratched below the surface it become clear that it believes in a version of 'trickledown' economics. Essentially, capital is seen as a progressive force and markets can be harnessed for good. So despite the playing up of the lack of internal competition and private finance in the NHS, the absence of academies and free schools, the presence free travel and personal care for the elderly and so on, the SNP supports capital (the employers) through state aid and market deregulation because it believes that if it allows capital to grow, to invest and to increase its profitability, this will provide a) the tax base – even at a lower rate – to generate the necessary funds for its social programmes, and b) increase employment, requiring less dependency upon the welfare state. But not only is this not likely under a sustained period of economic stagnation in the global north but past experience shows that welfare is always cut when profits fall – and falling profits are a recurring phenomenon under capitalism. Even if it were at all possible, the SNP has made it clear that there are very definite limits to its ambitions for social welfare. These consists of maintaining the current level of provision – therefore, not expanding it or making it better – when it has been shown to be increasingly inadequate as cuts are made in welfare provision and as the real value of benefits is undermined by inflation. The way this comes out in practice is that the SNP's vision of independence is only to turn the clock back on reforms to the welfare state since the Coalition government came into power in 2010 and ignore all the attacks that took place under the Blair and Brown Labour governments.

    In short, the SNP envisages building a Scottish version of the former
Irish 'tiger' economy with lower corporation tax. Indeed, cutting corporation
tax in this will actually stimulate the race to the bottom with other countries
as competition exists to attract the overseas investment to Scotland in the
first place. So, the SNP is committed to political - not social – change but
even here this is little radicalism. The monarchy and sterling will remain
and defence will be part of a shared services approach with England (within
NATO). But there is worse. Wishing to continue to be part of the sterling
currency zone and giving the Bank of England the right to set interest
rates shows that the SNP wants to continue to hitch the fate of those in the
economy in Scotland to the decisions of neo-liberal institutions in London
and elsewhere like New York, Frankfurt and Brussels. The fact that it does not
even seek to gain the levers for an independent state that would allow it to
make these key economic and financial decisions in Scotland indicates just
how timid and conservative the SNP is. Put bluntly, the SNP does not want
these powers because it sees no need for them. Indeed, when you consider
the very marked limitations to the SNP's vision of independence, it begs
the question 'why bother?' for so little will change under it. 'Conservative'
rather than 'moderate' is the best categorisation of the SNP. Again there is
worse when one ponders the significance of the SNP's vision. It is not even
an 'indie lite' one but a vision of federalism and 'devo max' for with such
shared institutions (monetary, fiscal, military) and a lack of the full tools of
independence, the SNP is determined not to offer full independence as an
option in the referendum.

    Yet the conservatism of the SNP runs deeper still. When asked by Cat
Boyd, a prominent activist in the PCS union at the first annual lecture of the
Jimmy Reid Foundation in January 2013 if the SNP would abolish the anti-
unions laws in an independent Scotland, Alex Salmond gave the following
response: 'it would be up to the Parliament to decide'. As a statement of fact,
that is no doubt true but what it represented was an attempt to avoid giving
a specific response and especially one where the SNP is not prepared to
abolish the anti-unions laws. A desirable response from Salmond would have
been along the lines of 'Yes, the SNP will do its utmost to secure a majority
to abolish these Tory anti-union laws. And the reason the SNP will do so is as
an attempt to restore some semblance of balance in power between capital
and labour.' That Salmond did not is an indication of his and the SNP's
underlying belief in trickledown economics. Hence, not only is capital to
be left unrestricted in its operations in order to make its investments which
then helps creates the jobs and the tax revenue base but the state is very
much 'open for business'. This means that state sees its role to facilitate this
investment by offering a number of financial subsidies on rent, training and
so on. At base, this policy is one of welcoming new jobs in the economy
without regard for the pay and conditions of the workers in these jobs. If

the SNP was genuinely concerned about the multiplier effect in terms of its ability to provide sustained economic growth with an accompanying fair distribution of wealth, it would be concerned about the nature of the new jobs being created and that need to be created. The example of Amazon is instructive.

Under an SNP government, Amazon's various investments in building and expanding its facilities in Scotland have been warmly welcomed. The company is well known to be an anti-union and has maintained this stance in its operations in Scotland – for example, a worker at the Gourock plant claimed his working life was made intolerable after he tried and failed to get a union representative to accompany him to an internal meeting and the GMB union has been refused entry to the company's premises. This worker's career suffered after he made his union affiliation known. The worker then resigned after a series of run-ins with management following his attempts to be represented by his union and he took his case to an employment tribunal in Scotland, claiming union victimisation and constructive dismal. *The Herald* (26 February 2011) obtained internal Amazon papers that showed the company's most senior manager in Gourock failed to rule out repercussions for workers who joined a union. A manager, speaking to a meeting of all employees at the warehouse in 2010, was asked directly if there would be consequences for those workers who join a union. He replied: 'I can't say whether there would or wouldn't be repercussions. Amazon prefers to consult with its employees through other means'.

Amazon is also not known to be a provider of particularly good pay or working conditions (*Herald* 13 December 2010). In the run up to Christmas 2010, the company in Gourock cut short the shifts of casual staff in the middle of the night and without any notice, leaving some workers who were reliant upon public transport to get home to wait until the resumption of services the following morning. No compensation was paid to these casual workers for neither cutting their shifts short nor for the inconvenience caused. Their hourly rate is only just above the minimum wage.

These two instances with Amazon are just small indications that the SNP has no concern for the quality of the jobs or the conditions workers are employed on. Rather, the SNP seems to think that all new jobs are necessarily 'good' jobs, no matter their purpose, conditions, prospects or security. But Salmond and the SNP could choose to use certain levers they have to (through investment policy and enterprise grants) to insist upon a living wage for workers, no use of zero-hour contracts and so on as a conditions for any new investment[5]. They could also insist upon union recognition being a condition of companies being eligible for receipt of public funds. For example, Amazon received £2.5m in Scottish Enterprise grants to establish its Dunfermline operation. So, as with Amazon as with other new investment, whether domestic or overseas, the SNP has shown no willingness or ability to enforce that employment should be based on full-time, permanent jobs where wages are sufficiently high as to not have a working poor. Indeed, a working poor represents the state subsidy of employers paying low wages because workers have to claim working family tax credits in an attempt to make ends meet.

Changing the leopard's spots?

Of late, there seems to be evidence that the SNP is moving to the left. Extrapolating from this, some believe this is just the beginning of a more fulsome journey so that the SNP becomes even more progressive. One example of this is Salmond's pledge that in an independent Scotland, there would be a constitutional right to a home and there would be a right to employment or training for the young. Another is that the SNP has moved to end the right of council tenants to buy their houses. A third is that the age of retirement will be reduced from 68 to 67 under independence. Let's not be churlish – these are welcome moves. But there is more to say. First, without a taxation system (and a progressive one at that) in place that can generate the necessary resources to provide the housing – and adequate housing at that – the right on paper will not amount to a much of a right in practice. Moreover, the end of the right to buy will not come into effect until 2017. Applying the same type of logic to the right to employment or training, the right will only be worthwhile if employers are forced to provide it and not given, in effect, state subsidies to taken on low waged workers. The political nature of the SNP is such that it is a safer bet that it would not take these necessary steps. On the issue of pensions, the inability or unwillingness to reduce the age of retirement back to 65 shows how timid and moderate the SNP is as well as how its misses a trick in terms of winning much wider support for independence.

Elsewhere, and when the SNP makes progressive noises, there is a large dose of political opportunism at work. For example, the SNP hinted after George Osborne's 2013 spending review that it would not abolish increments for public sector workers. But it made no corollary about where it would find the money for this, effectively negating the hint. Another instance is over the record of the SNP governments over public sector redundancies. The SNP frequently and proudly proclaims that it has a no compulsory redundancy policy. It does and it has kept its word. But that is only half the story because it also has a policy of voluntary redundancies and non-replacement in order to reduce spending. This means that thousands of jobs have been shed and services have been cut as staffing numbers have been reduced.

All this speaks to the wholly inadequate political pitch of the SNP – vote for independence to stop things getting a bit worse, whether it be the social wage or NHS. Thus, the SNP's vision is not about making things better or even about reversing the situation. In government, especially from 2011 onwards, the SNP has been about making small, incremental improvement which fall far, far short of meeting the social need that exists. Even in the year of the referendum, Finance Secretary, John Swinney, kept to this script with his 2014-2015 budget, saying his spending plans would merely 'limit the damage of Westminster's welfare cuts'.

The alternative to the SNP: a new party of left?

To say that the SNP cannot be relied upon – or, indeed, used – to deliver a radical version of independence is to necessarily suggest that another or other political forces to the left need to exist and for them to play a decisive role. Unfortunately, we are in the unenviable position of trying to re-invent the wheel in a very short space of time. We know that if the Scottish Socialist Party (SSP) had not imploded as a result of Tommy Sheridan's actions over trying to disprove what was true about his sex life, the SSP would be in a strong position to provide not just the leadership of but also the ballast for the radical pro-independence forces. Representation in the Scottish Parliament prior to 2014 (the 2007-2011 parliament, the 2011- parliament) would have allowed the socialist case to be made in the public debate and for the left to coalesce around this parliamentary force because with it would come profile and standing. But we are all very well aware that this was not - and is not - the case. We can only play the hand we have been dealt. This means that the existing but diminished SSP and the forces around the Radical Independence Campaign (especially the International Socialist Group) have a critical responsibility to step up to the plate to form some kind of coherent and credible organisation that can present itself as a political vehicle through which the aspirations and demands of the left and oppositional social movements can be operationalized inside the parliamentary system. That process of re-alignment and renewal needs to get underway as soon as possible and be in place well in advance of the 2016 Scottish Parliament elections so that the prospect of attaining representation in that parliament is a serious one. If the left can do this, it can hope to attract some from the SNP – both MSPs and activists – because while the SNP will not breakup or implode anytime soon after independence, it is likely to begin to fracture and fragment around the edges.

The STUC and unions

Most unions and the STUC are extremely unlikely to support independence – especially because they argue that it will be shaped by the SNP. They may not support the Union either – given that it is a neo-liberal Union defined by Labour and the Tories. But that is to cede unnecessary ground to the SNP because the STUC and its affiliates could alternatively say to the SNP that the case for independence could be supported if it looks like 'x' and not 'y'. In other words, they could say that the price for any support for independence must be predicated on independence looking like 'x'. This requires a far more pro-active and bargaining-type of stance than has been shown so far. Since 2012, the STUC and the major unions like Unite and Unison have essentially toyed with the Yes Scotland campaign by asking questions of it which can then inform their members' views. Fine as far as it goes but there's little sense of attempting to support those within Yes Scotland that favour a radical form of independence against those that do not. If the STUC, in particular, maintains its current line, it will forgo the opportunity to influence any independence outcome in the way that it was central to the creation of devolution.

Conclusion

Since attaining the position of a majority government in May 2011, the SNP has increasingly become a liability to the very goal that it as a party was set up to achieve. Its cautious and conservative approach has no ability to set the heather alight for citizens that want to see a society in Scotland based upon an equality of outcomes in people's lives. This is because radical change is beyond what the SNP is capable of, whether it be in the form of wealth redistribution through the tax system or in the form of the financial and economic regulation of the business interests of the rich and powerful[6]. Ironically despite Salmond's failed attempt to get a second question on the ballot paper for the referendum (as per the Edinburgh Agreement of 15 October 2012), Salmond has in effect made sure this is still the option on offer from the SNP by fashioning his version of 'indie lite' to be a combination of 'devo max' and federalism. The phrase that 'independence is a process not an event' takes on a new and different meaning with the SNP's aforementioned strategy. The radical left strategy outlined in this book is certainly a forthright exposition of independence being a process not an event. But the SNP's interpretation of it is as a way to stave off social change because it is not party of radicals and it does not wish to face down the rich and powerful. To force the pace and build up a head of steam for radical independence, the left needs to not only organise itself much better than it ever has been in recent years but also start operating in a way that wins hearts and minds well beyond its own ranks.

Chapter 6: Red Herrings

Introduction

There are a number of red herrings in the debate within the left about what the consequences of and motivations for independence. This chapter examines the major ones. First is the equation of independence with nationalism. Second is the charge that independence will split the unity of the working class in Britain. Third is the notion an independent Scotland would see the peoples of England consigned to permanent Tory rule.

Independence and nationalism

Supporting independence and self-determination does not make one a nationalist as the writings of Marx and Lenin, amongst others, make clear. So to universally equate independence with nationalism is facile in the extreme. Whether the two are synonymous very much depends upon the circumstances and situation[7]. In the case of Scotland, there is very little evidence of anyone on the left i) advocating that there are truly intra-nation-based solutions to inter-national social and economic problems; ii) denying antagonistic interests of different social classes by seeking to unite citizens by nationality; and iii) assuming that one nation is superior to another leading to competition and rivalry. Within the SNP, there are certainly strains of the first two (but not the third) but even here we do not face a situation similar to the Czechs wanting to split from the Slovaks because the Czechs were the richer nation and did not want to 'subsidise' the Slovaks any more. There is no sense of national grievance against England and the English, whether out of economic oppression, much less political or cultural oppression. Far more importantly, to equate independence with nationalism is to not only misunderstand what internationalism is but also to fail to comprehend the progressive role that struggles for independence can have.

The standard, sloganised retort from the Unionist left to anyone supporting independence is 'I'm an internationalist – not a nationalist'. This has been the case since at least the 1960s for Jimmy Reid remarked upon the use of the very phrase in his *Reflections of a Clydebuilt Man* (1976, p116).

The problem with the Unionist retort exists on a number of levels. First, the internationalism proclaimed is not inter-nationalism but, in fact, trans-nationalism. Transnationalism is a creed that does not recognise the worth of nations and national identity in all their various forms and differences. It seeks to deny such national differences and, instead, proclaims that workers of the world have no righteous identity other than that of class. Second, inter-nationalism is that of between nations – it is about the relationship between nations, whether as the present actual or future intended relationship. Third, it then makes sense to see that inter-nationalism cannot be counter-posed to nationalism. But even more crucially, nationalism is viewed as a particular form and type of political expression, namely, that of being competitive against other nations, even chauvinistic, uniting the classes of capital (the ruling class) and labour (the working class) together in an unholy alliance that only benefits the former, and attempting to find local solutions to global problems that cannot be solved at a local level. Those who support independence from the left are not nationalists in any shape or form. Rather, they seek to give expression and representation to the social values that underpin a radical notion of national identity – i.e., what it means to be 'Scottish' – by creating the political space for this to happen through the establishment of an independent state in Scotland. In doing so, the hope is that localised action can be part of a more global trend towards ending the domination of capital and its ideology of neo-liberalism. 'Thinking globally, acting locally' and trying to set a useful example by beginning a radical social experiment are the basic perspectives.

Without wishing to overstate the parallel, there is no intrinsic problem working for the same intermediate end as other political forces provided that your eyes are as wide open as possible. Scottish-born socialist, James Connolly, said to his members in the Irish Citizen Army on 16 April 1916 - just over a week before the uprising: 'The odds are a thousand to one against us, but in the event of victory, hold onto your rifles, as those with whom we are fighting may stop before our goal is reached.' The lesson to be taken forward here is neither to abandon criticism of the SNP before the referendum nor cease to make the arguments for radical independence (and building up those forces) for as much metaphorical ammunition as possible will be needed should independence be won and under the SNP's leadership.

Splitting the working class?

One of the standard but also most damning arguments on the left against independence is that a) it would break the unity and strength of the unions and working class in Britain, and b) that this unity and strength is predicated on organisational structures being cross-British. It is made by the likes of left-wing Labour MSP, Neil Findlay, and GMB Scotland political officer, Richard Leonard. This is, indeed, a serious accusation which then warrants a serious examination to see whether it stands up to critique and holds any water. So what would such a cataclysm look like and what are its prospects? The first consequence in this scenario would be that common employers are not faced by workers by in the same union or as a joint force so that workers are weaker and ultimately can be subject to the tactic of 'divide and rule' by employers. The second is that workers do not show solidarity to each other when they are in struggle because they no longer see themselves as brothers and sisters due to the border. The third is that workers compete against each other – on their terms and conditions of employment – in order to win the favour of employers.

Each of these is more than possible if Scotland was to become independent. But that does not mean to say that they are probable because it is seldom that the structure of unions in and of itself - within and between different countries - plays a decisive or significant role. What is more important factor is the oppositional class consciousness of workers. Such a consciousness can lead to different workers in different unions in different countries pulling or pushing in the same direction. For example, the 1984-1985 miners' strike saw huge financial donations from outside Britain (especially from French, Russian and East European miners) as well as huge divisions within Britain especially in the form of the Nottinghamshire area of the NUM. That the NUM was a British-wide union did not have a bearing on this. The same point is true of the Liverpool dockers' strike of 1995-1996. The more substantial support was forthcoming from dockers outside Britain and not the dockers own union, the TGWU. Nonetheless, workers in the same industries in different and the same countries can and do already compete against each other in order to receive investment for continued production at their workplaces. The most obvious example here is of car companies ranking their various plants in an inter-national productivity league table and only further investing in the most productive ones and closing down the least productive ones. So some care needs to be taken in order not to wrongly assume that change in the structure of nation states means that worker solidarity across borders cannot or will not take place. But by the same token, it should not be assumed that bigger states guarantee that unions within them will support their members in struggles throughout the geographical territory of the state.

The strongest case for such a doomsday scenario of disunity is probably to be found in the public sector/public services (see below) and not in the private sector. This is because there would be little to no change to structure of employers in the private sector but much in the public sector. In the private sector, there is no reason for workers to either leave existing unions to set up new ones, or for existing unions not to cooperate with each other either side of the border if Scotland was to become independent. This is because regardless of a new border, the employers in the private sector would pretty much remain the same compared to how they were before. Yes, employers would be constituted as separate legal companies in Scotland given that they would be operating in a new state while continuing as before south of the border. But the close historic and on-going ties either side of the border suggest that in practice the companies would continue to act pretty much as one body either side of the border, especially as the existing management would remain in place. This point is buttressed by the fact that employment law in an independent Scotland is unlikely to change (and change dramatically) any time soon under an SNP-dominated government. But more important than this would be that the structure of the labour market within the Britain would remain very similar because workers are prepared to move across and throughout Britain for work and because employers would recruit throughout Britain for employment north and south of the border. So, for workers employed in effectively the same company either side of the border, there would be no point not staying in the same union. Again this point is buttressed by the fact that existing structures of collective bargaining would be anticipated to stay the same with cross-border negotiations the norm. Thus, workers in the same company either side of the border would continue under company-level or industry-level negotiations to bargain together collectively with their common employer(s). Where competition in the private sector is possible between workers either side of the border between England and Scotland is over competition for investment and to escape divestment. This would not be a new phenomenon as competition already exists between different areas within Britain to attract investment or retain production (especially by offering concessions on work practices).

What would be new would be that corporation tax levels could be significantly lower in Scotland than in England (or Wales and Northern Ireland) as this is the intention of the SNP. Indeed, the SNP has stated that it intends to reduce corporation tax the level of the Republic of Ireland. That reduction might occasion workers in England to feel compelled to offer concessions in their terms and conditions of employment in order to counter-balance what was perceived as Scotland's competitive advantage (i.e., to make up for the higher taxes in England). Or it might compel the government in the rest of Britain to lower its corporation tax (or change the tax law so that companies find it easier to evade paying their full amount of corporation tax).

The situation in the public sector is probably much different though. A new state in Scotland will become a new employer for many public sector workers, occasioning new and separate bargaining arrangements. Already significant numbers of civil servants are employed by the Scottish government and covered by separate collective bargaining arrangements. Furthermore, teachers, local government workers are, for example, already covered by separate collective bargaining arrangements in Scotland compared to south of the border. Only in teaching are there already separate unions (although the NASUWT organises north and south of the border). Yet there remains much similarity here in terms of wage structures and associated conditions because of the existence of a Britain-wide labour market. And it should be noted that other than the case with the EIS (which is affiliated to the TUC), Unison and PCS organise these workers already either side of the existing border.

But those public sector workers which would be employed by a new (state) employer would be the majority of those in the civil service. One could foresee a situation, with a state as employer which has its own policy objectives and a different path for national development, where members of existing unions in the civil service may not feel quite so compelled to remain in the same unions as those for civil servants in England. But before this conclusion could be reached, these civil servants opting for cession would have to be of the view that a) their existing Britain-wide union was not prepared to give them sufficient autonomy to be able to deal with the different situation in Scotland[8]; b) the labour markets north and south of the border were sufficiently different for civil servants that a common union was of no great benefit; and c) employment law would diverge between the two countries so that Scotland became much more progressive than it was in England. It is hard to see these three conditions being fulfilled, especially as it is not anticipated that an independent Scotland under the SNP would create significantly better conditions for civil servants. So both employer and bargaining structures would diverge but that would not mean that new and different unions would be required, much less be desirable. Indeed, if a union like the PCS has policies – and implements these – based upon resisting neo-liberalism and austerity, then there is no reason to believe that civil servants in an independent Scotland would not also want a union able to have and implement the same policies under a new state.

In addition to the civil servants, the ending of national (i.e., Britain-wide) bargaining in the fire service and universities could be expected. Already there have been longstanding pressures from employers to end this form of bargaining in the universities but a new opportunity would arise with independence. The pressure for ending national bargaining in the fire service has been less marked. Nonetheless, what employers in both sectors wish is to move to forms of regional bargaining (or especially in case of universities sub-national bargaining like cartels of institutions of similar standing) where pay and conditions can either reflect different geographical labour markets or different amounts of resources. Yet the question of whether this would lead to new, separate unions is very much open to doubt for the reasons raised above with regard to the civil service. But in this instance, existing membership of the same unions in the fire service and universities is also likely to be maintained because downward pressure on terms and conditions of employment could arise in either or both England and Scotland. Maintenance of membership of the same union would be a helpful step to resisting such downward pressure

To re-iterate the point made earlier, being in the same union is no guarantee of action as the structure of unions is not the key determining factor. Rather, oppositional consciousness is. That said, there is little prospect when the scenarios are thought through of independence in Scotland either in the public or private sectors occasioning the creation of new Scottish-only unions as a result of cession from existing British-wide unions. But there is also another factor that needs to be borne in mind – this is the pressing need for.

We also need to be aware of the historical experience and precedent. First, the creation of the Irish Free State in 1921 did not prevent unions like the TGWU, MSF, Amicus, UCATT, the TSSA and the NUJ and their fore bearers from operating as all-Britain unions. It does not prevent the Unite union – the successor to the TGWU, MSF and Amicus - today from doing so either and the NUJ and TSSA continue to do so too. These unions established structures and processes to allow for sufficient autonomy and resources so that members' interests could be pursued under their all-Britain structures[9]. The belief in strength in numbers and unity is strength was not torn apart by the creation of the Irish Free State. Second, the last highpoint of truly historic recent working class unity which meant something because it was not only a mass mobilisation but was successful (partially at least) was the revolt against the poll tax. The revolt started in Scotland, with modus operandi of revolt and resistance exported to England. Before this, we can recall the mass mobilisation around the 1984-1985 miners' strike and before that the various struggles in 1972 including the battle against the Industrial Relations Act 1971. Thus, it's a hard case to argue that the union movement today is in a healthy, vibrant state or on the verge of an upturn in struggle so the sense that the strength or unity (bringing about strength) could be rendered ineffective by the emergence of an independent Scotland is not a convincing one[10].

All this is important context because one way of approaching the independence debate is to see the issues in terms of tactics and strategy rather than in terms of principles and ideology. So if mobilised working class unity on an all-Britain basis is not anywhere near a highpoint because of a decline in class consciousness and the capability to collectively mobolise, we should then ask are there other ways to get to where we want to be? In other words, could an independent Scotland help push and prod workers south of the border into a re-awakening of a progressive or class consciousness? And, would unions necessarily have to change in order to operate both sides of the border? If workers in Britain can take inspiration from what workers do elsewhere in the world as workers and citizens, whether this be Egypt, Venezuela or America, there is no reason why workers should not take inspiration in England from what workers do in Scotland.

England with permanent Tory rule?

One of the (minor) arguments against a vote for independence is that it would leave England dominated by a permanent Tory majority because Labour in Westminster would be denied its 40-odd seats that it could rely on gaining in Scotland. On this basis, the counter-argument is constructed that it would be an act of solidarity to vote against independence. This is a daft argument on a number of levels. First, out of a sense of desperation, it suggests there is little hope of the majority of voters in England either supporting Labour or a more radical version of it than which is on offer currently. But it does so in the absence of Labour moving to the left and putting up a widespread and sustained opposition to the Tories. It is a reasonable proposition to suggest that if Labour did this it would become more popular amongst the mass of citizens to be found in the working class (albeit losing support among some groups in the middle class). On this basis, it could command a majority of parliamentary seats for England. Second, and by way of illustration with the anti-poll tax rebellion, developments in Scotland can have a positive demonstration impact upon England. The poll tax was introduced a year earlier into Scotland (in 1989) than in England and the earlier organisation of dissent there showed what was possible to those south of the border. Indeed, Tommy Sheridan was in great demand as a speaker down south at this time. In the same way, independence in Scotland could help trigger a reassessment of what the nature of both the form and nature of politics in England should be – a parliament for England might be one outcome or regional assemblies would be another. This might then stimulate demands and campaigns that would allow the neo-liberal stranglehold at Westminster to be challenged. In addition, fuller devolution in or independence for Wales would also become a fuller prospect, and here (as with Scotland's central belt) the more left inclined views of south Wales would be allowed to be expressed in a way that would move the political centre of gravity to the left. Third, the arithmetic of parliament suggests that there have only been two occasions in the past when a Labour victory at Westminster would have been turned into a Tory government if Scotland had been independent. These were the 1964 and February 1974 general elections. In 2010, all parties were denied/denied themselves an absolute majority, with the Tories forming a coalition with the Liberal Democrats. The absence of 41 Labour MPs would not seem to have altered the fact that the Tories would be in power – either as a minority government or as the lead partner in a coalition. This, therefore, is hardly the stuff of Scots uncaringly subjecting their brothers and sisters south of the border to interminable years of Tory rule.

Conclusion

Common cause based on common interests can lead to common action. But it is the political understanding, consciousness and will that form the basis of the unity in action and not the institutions, organisations and structures themselves. This chapter has made clear that workers employed by companies and organisations operating north and south of a future border between Scotland and England will still need to be in the same union as each other in order to effectively prosecute their collective interests. Indeed, workers in the same sectors and industries will still need to be in the same unions as before if Scotland becomes independent. Now more than ever the principle of union organisation is to organise across borders because capital is organised across borders too. So the concern – and challenge – is not about whether there will be separate unions north and south of the Scottish-English border but, rather, about how can inter-national unions be created, especially for workers in the private sector in countries in continental Europe and north America. This is because in an ever more globalised and integrated world economy, workers' unity is needed and this is not predicted upon structures and organisational shapes but political will, collective confidence and political values. The search for the inter- and trans-national unity of workers in action goes back at least as far as Karl Marx's involvement in the International Workingmen's Association in the 1860s.

Chapter 7: Limits to social change under independence

Introduction

There are distinct limits to the extent to which 'Scottish solutions' can solve problems in Scotland – Scottish or otherwise - because the Scottish economy is very much part of a capitalist world economy and subject to the same dynamics and ebbs and flows as other parts of the global economy. There can be no total shield in Scotland alone from the effects of capitalism, its neo-liberal moment and the age of austerity. Only some form of autarky could establish otherwise, and previous experiments in autarky have not been pleasant to say the least. Experiments of 'socialism in one country' or 'national paths to socialism' have involved compromises with capital as well as internal sacrifices and repression. Thus, a sustained, embedded and more full-blooded programme of social change then requires that similar moves towards forms of social liberation take place in other countries which mutually support each other and prevent the isolation of radical social experiments. Cooperation between progressive nations and societies rather than competition between them and acquiescence to global capitalism is required to support and strengthen developments in Scotland. This, therefore, cuts across the SNP's fanciful notion that independence will give political and economic sovereignty to Scotland as a state and to the people that reside in it – or to put it in Salmond's speak 'that decisions about what happens in Scotland are always taken by the people who live and work here' as he told the rally for independence on 21 September 2013.

Integration and inter-dependence

The economy of Scotland (as well as and Britain as a whole) has always been well-integrated into the world economy. Dating back to the times of the slave trade and then heyday of shipbuilding and heavy engineering on Clydeside, Glasgow was the second city of the British Empire. Although Glasgow experienced severe deindustrialisation, Edinburgh flowered as a financial centre. Alongside this, many American and Japanese companies invested in Scotland. Today, the Royal Bank of Scotland is emblematic of the extent to which a nominally Scottish company is a major player in the world economy (notwithstanding its near collapse in 2008 and subsequent bailing out with public funds). But whether companies that operate in Scotland or are headquartered in Scotland are leading ones is immaterial because the extent of the integration and inter-dependence of the Scottish economy with the world economy is based on a) trade between these different economic areas (especially with the countries of the European Union); b) the inter-nationalisation of the supply chain where companies operating in Scotland supply assemblers and assemble themselves; and c) the general level of economic activity in the world economy (boom or slump most obviously) has a significant bearing on the levels of demand and supply in Scotland (and elsewhere). With this the integration and inter-dependence comes the domination of the transnational social (capitalist) class that owns, controls and benefits from the means of production, distribution and exchange. This class – not withstanding some rivalry and competition – has colonised the institutions and government of the world economy with the ideology of neo-liberalism. These institutions are the International Monetary Fund, World Bank, European Central Bank, European Commission, various free trade agreements and so on. These institutions have pioneered the opening up of new areas of society and news regions of the world to the full operation of the free market. At the same time, this organisation of this class has become more concentrated and centralised through the growth of major conglomerates. The growth of the BRICs (Brazil, Russia, India and China) has merely altered the locus and configuration of this phenomenon not its existence and means of operation. The consequence of this is that any attempts to institute the pursuit of social justice and an equality of outcomes in Scotland – small as Scotland is – will not be viewed favourably. Indeed, they are more likely to be viewed with hostility (especially if the removal of Trident is a counterpart to this). No special favours of help and support will be forthcoming. Indeed, sanctions, disinvestment and capital strikes could be the response from capital and the international institutions of capitalism. And the effect of these would be deepened when there is next recession – as there will inevitably be.

So in order to try to withstand and offset the force of these anticipated measures, an independent Scotland will need to work with and ally with other progressive forces elsewhere in Europe and further afield to create a counter-balance. The would concern not only sharing resources and forming political alliances to outflank the forces of reaction but also benefitting from attempts by domestic social forces within their own different nation states to stop their own governments and ruling classes from acting in certain detrimental ways by imposing economic and political costs upon them. This is clearly a tall order and much in the way of arriving at such a situation is outside the control of an independent Scotland. But not trying to do so is the surest way to failure. The best way of helping to get to the desired point is for an independent Scotland to be progressive not only in foreign and overseas development policies but to mindfully progressive in the external implications of what happens internally. For example, policy on immigration would be one example. But there is a further aspect that bear repeating albeit for a different purpose - if a future Scottish economy was based primarily upon attracting foreign investment (whether for manufacturing or services), then it would necessarily be more susceptible to the aforementioned pressures of reaction. If, however, the economy in Scotland had at its centre a large sector of cooperatives, mutuals and other forms of socialised ownership, then there would not be the same susceptibility. Such a type of economy does exist in the Basque country in Spain with the Mondragon organisation of cooperatives (see before). The issue of the flight of capital would be less pressing as would be making concessions to attract investment in the first place.

Conclusion

Only with 'indie max' giving the fullest levers of power - and these then being used to their full extent – can progress be made towards solving the economic and social ills found in Scotland. But it has to be also fully understood that all of Scotland's economic and social ills cannot be solved and resolved within Scotland because it is part of a globalised capitalist system. Yet, this is not the quite the case of the Russian Revolution of October 1917 being strangled from the outside by foreign armies supporting the White Army against the Red Army. But there is a parallel in the isolation of the Russian Revolution when the German Revolution of 1918 to 1923 was misdirected and brutally suppressed – developments in one country that challenge the status quo cannot last for long or be particularly victorious without the successful spread of the challenge to other countries in order to re-order the balance of forces. It is the enmeshing together of the internal and external processes in a mutually supportive way that is required in order to furnish success and advance. That is why the next chapter examines not just the potentially positive impact that independence for Scotland could have but also why any success towards this will be reliant to some extent upon other countries creating a conducive environment for the radical social experiment in Scotland. But the enmeshing together of the internal and external processes in a mutually supportive way is also required to stop Scotland being part of a 'race to bottom' by adding to the number of countries that compete for inward investment on the basis of labour costs (see chapter 6).

Chapter 8: A boon to – not a barrier for - others

Introduction

The example of Scotland not only going its own way but also travelling down a radical road would have positive, progressive implications beyond the boundaries of Scotland itself. Most obviously, this would concern the rest of the nations of the British Isles but it might also include the likes of Catalonia and the Basque Country. This chapter considers the ramifications for the generalisation of the progressive politics out with Scotland. It does not make the claim that the impact of radical independence for Scotland would be anything on a par with the impact of the Chavez-led Bolivarian revolution in Venezuela upon Latin America. Rather, the suggestion is a measured and sensible one. That said, it is only if the direction of travel for independence is of the kind that is outlined in this book that Scotland could in any way become a progressive beacon. Therefore, Alex Salmond considerably overegged his pudding by saying in January 2012 that an independent Scotland could be such a progressive beacon for others because he is set against the very measures that could allow this to happen.

England

There are several major implications and spurs to potential political change. The first is that the appeal of the right in the form of the UK Independence Party (UKIP) and the xenophobic Tory right could be cut down to size. At the moment, these reactionary forces have a popular appeal because they seem to articulate the grievances of many citizens in England. The support of the discontented for these political forces is misplaced but that situation has been arrived at because there is no credible left to take the anger in a different direction. The second is that if political power can be devolved to a population the size of Scotland, there is no reason why this cannot happen in a meaningful and popular way to the regions of England. The major regions could then have their own assemblies or parliaments so that England became a federation where the Westminster parliament played a coordinating role for the devolved parliaments. The third, and accompanying this, is that the political domination of the south of England over the north of England could be ended and, in this situation, a more progressive set of political policies implemented. The fourth is that the left in England would be given a kick up the arse to sort itself out as new forces emerged to not just demand but create a broader, more credible and less sectarian left. The Left Unity project, initiated by Ken Loach's call, is one indication of the fertile ground from which this development could emerge. Indeed, it was not so long ago that the Scottish Socialist Party (SSP) provided the inspiration to the establishment of the Socialist Alliance in England so some cross border cross-fertilisation could be envisaged again. The fifth, and final, spur is that if union strength and mobilisation in Scotland were evident and effective, then with the close remaining links with fellow union members south of the border, a demonstration effect might be set in train, whereby those in unions in England became more confident and willing to try to emulate their counterparts north of the border. But one of the key issues in all of this is not just what is done but also who it is done by. Thus, a critical test is that workers' promote their own (left) agenda and have success in doing so in all of this. If organised workers can establish that the 'new' Scotland is one where the state and other bodies intervene to ameliorate the processes and outcomes of the market – and stop the further encroachment of the market into other parts of society – then this will be a key achievement. It should lead to workers in England asking why they are not doing similarly.

Wales

After the very close run vote (50.3%: 49.7%) for a more limited form of devolution in Wales in 1997, the demand for further devolution has increased. In 2011, by a margin of 63%:37%, a referendum voted to enhance the powers for the Welsh Assembly. And while demand for further devolution is not the same as demand for independence, there is likely to be a) many within the pro-devolution camp that wish to go further, namely, gain independence; and b) many that over time would come to see independence as a further elaboration upon devolution in terms of what can be decided in Cardiff rather than elsewhere. The establishment of 'clear red water' – the phrase coined by Welsh First Minister, Rhodri Morgan, in 2002 to describe the growing policy divergence between Labour governments in Cardiff and Westminster in the early 2000s - indicates that there is a wellspring of radicalism that could be tapped into and not just further articulated but also see it gain influence in an environment where independence became more of a prospect. Scottish independence could easily help play a major in this process.

Spain

There are reasonably close but far from precise parallels between the movements for cession from the Spanish state by Catalonia and the Basque country, on the one hand, and Scotland, on the other. Contact between the left pro-independence forces in Scotland and these parts of Spain suggests that the latter would draw some further solace from a 'yes' vote (even if the cession mobilisations in Catalonia have by numerical size far outstripped any in Scotland). Moreover, the Spanish government has voiced its opinion that Scotland would not become an automatic member of the EU in order to stymie the movement towards Catalonian cession.

Trident

On a range of issues of wealth redistribution and equality of outcomes, the ripple effect of Scotland becoming a far more social democratically inclined country in a neo-liberal world may not be as substantial outside of the British Isles as that of removing Trident and nuclear weapons from Scottish soil and waters. Whilst the Nordic countries have retreated from their social democratic highpoint of the post-war period (Sweden especially), they still remain sufficiently different as coordinated market economies (rather than liberal market economies) to stand out so that this takes the edge off what the wider significance of an independent Scotland would represent. This is not true on Trident because of the significance of the nuclear weapons for NATO and the US. While Denmark and Norway are NATO members and Sweden and Finland are not, it is the siting of such strategically important weapons in one of the few inlets that can accommodate them within territory of the most fervent supporter of the US that is the crux of the matter. The significance of the impact of removing Trident from Scottish waters is magnified by the difficulty of finding another suitable coastal base elsewhere in the British Isles.

Conclusion

It is only some kind of self-induced Scottish cringe that could deny there is at least some possibility that Scotland could serve as a progressive example to other peoples and nations elsewhere. We can argue over how strong the push and pull of this might be but we should not discount it per se. But for there to be any push or pull requires that Scotland as a society is much more radical than Alex Salmond ever intends. At the same time, we also need to remain mindful that not all social questions have the answer of independence because battles need to be fought in the here and now – and these are equally capable of having a positive demonstration beyond the shores of Scotland.

Chapter 9: Conclusion

Introduction

Despite the SNP bringing about the opportunity of the referendum on 18 September 2014, it is not a political force either capable of winning the referendum for a 'yes' nor of doing so on a progressive basis. As a political force, it has continually sought to deploy the weakness of arguments for independence, namely, for the democratic right of self-determination and not for the strongest of arguments, namely, what using the full levers of independence could and should deliver in order to significantly reduce poverty and social inequality. In other words, it has fixated on the means and not the ends. Salmond is particularly guilty of this and Sturgeon has not managed to act as any great counter-weight to this. Notwithstanding all this, independence does bring forth the possibility of creating lasting, substantial and progressive social change. This means, for example, not just ending austerity but reversing it. But this will be the responsibility of other political forces to the left of the SNP. For the radical left, the key issue is that independence will open up greater political space for left wing values to be represented within. The political centre of gravity in Scotland will provide the possibility of removing the influence of the neo-liberal political parties at Westminster even if it will not remove the influence of neo-liberalism at large (i.e., in world economy and amongst those at home).

So to centre the debate on the ends - and not the means - for independence is the key way to win supporters to a 'yes' vote and to then create a force to capable of pushing for this type of society under independence. This makes it clear that the radical left must present a strategy of a) at one and the same time arguing not just for independence but a certain type of independence and b) building the forces capable of delivering this as independence in and of itself will not do this. To win large numbers of working class voters to the 'yes' vote requires that the possibility of improving or resolving their social conditions (employment, education, health etc that make up the life chances of them and their families) is convincingly put at the heart of a 'yes' campaign. This means outlining a particular vision of independence and what a post-independent society in Scotland could/would then look like. At the very least, what is envisaged is a Scotland based upon the socialising of the processes and outcomes of market as per radical social democracy. Starting from this point – rather than any constitutional or political one – means that a certain type of pitch – i.e. content - needs to be made and this will clash with the SNP's vision of a neo- or social liberal Scotland. The radical case for independence will, thus, make plain what is independence will be for and what we what to be independent from. And, this clash with the ideology of the leadership of the SNP can be used to deepen and strengthen the purchase of the radical case for addressing the social conditions of the majority of citizens. In terms of the method of the pitch, it will have to relate existing conditions to credible solutions rather than talk in abstract or far flung ideas. Whether the democratised state or citizens' own voluntary organisations (or the particular mix of both) are the best means to achieve these social outcomes in something that can be debated.

The preceding perspective and analysis in this book is predicated upon a contingent assessment of the situation. Thus, the book does not begin from the starting point of a belief in the right of nations to self-determination. Instead, it begins from the position of how can significant social progress be achieved. Therefore, the approach to the issue of independence is contingent and instrumental and not ideological and of principal. Indeed, if two critical conditions existed, namely, that a) the level of class struggle throughout Britain was much higher and more successful than it has been for a long time, and b) the project to reclaim the Labour Party for the left by the affiliated unions showed any significant signs of being effective, then the calculation that social change is relatively more possible under independence would not hold. But as neither of these does exist (notwithstanding the attempt by Unite under Len McCluskey) and is unlikely to come into being in the short- to medium-term, the case for maintaining the Union is ultimately one of maintaining the status quo of neo-liberalism. And by the same token, to vote for independence is not synonymous with nationalism.

This is not socialism ... but might it help us get there?

Any critical reading of this book will conclude that what is being proposed – though radical – is not socialism, if socialism is defined (as it should be) as workers running society in their own interests - in other words, society organised by workers and for workers. This is true because the book is inherently and innately concerned with making reforms in citizens' material circumstances. It is not because socialism - as just defined - is seen as being irrelevant. Far from it. Rather, the argument presented here for radical social change and not socialism per se is merely because the mass consciousness and organisation of workers and citizens is not sufficiently oppositional and advanced as to make socialism anything like a credible prospect as an idea – much less a reality - at the moment or in the not-too-distant future. The question then becomes how can the current situation be advanced to this desired point, and the answer proffered here is that through the collective struggle for radical reforms this advance comes into prospect because the collective struggle required to gain the reforms will build capacity, confidence and consciousness. So the fight for betterment in the here and now can hopefully open up an avenue to the means to attain socialism. To pose it otherwise by making socialism the only goal in a take it or leave it manner of 'but that's not socialism' is not only puerile but unproductive. Fighting for reforms in the present is a valuable way for learning important lessons about contesting both the power of capital and the state even if to some that reeks of so-called 'reformism'.

Final comment

So will sufficient number of citizens in and of Scotland be brave enough to votes 'yes' on 18 September 2014, and do so in not just the knowledge that a 'yes' can lead to a radical Scotland if they play their part in collectively mobilising after the referendum to achieve this desired outcome? Time will most surely tell.

Notes

1. This was the case, for example, at the Yes Scotland launch in May 2012, the independence marches of September 2012 and September 2013 and the 2012 SNP conference. At least one positive thing can be said in this regard about Salmond – despite his involvement in '79 group', neither he nor anyone else has tried to give the misleading impression that the real 'socialist' Salmond will emerge once independence has been gained and the conservatism to get there is merely instrumental and not ideological.

2. Of course, this means that the campaigns themselves must be credible in a number of respects – united, inclusive, grounded and democratic. The experience of the emergence of various rival campaigns against the bedroom tax in Glasgow from late 2012 onwards shows that creating campaigns which have these features this is by no means an easy feat to achieve.

3. To the extent that there is coherence of organisation, this is the Yes Scotland campaign but that is also a weakness as it massively dominates the forces of independence with its rather timid approach to economic and social issues.

4. The SNP's statement on creating two oil funds (one for stabilisation, the other for long-term savings) after independence – while welcome – was insufficiently clear or robust for it did not establish what benefit to citizens they would bring not quantify any benefits. There was no sense of the boldness of the previous 'It's our oil' slogan. In connection to this, it is worth noting the SNP opposed Miliband's proposed cap on gas and electricity prices of September 2013.

5. Indeed, the SNP's Procurement Reform Bill of late 2013 did not require contractors to pay the 'living wage', and in the guidance for the Bill, it was left up to the individual public bodies concerned as to whether they outlawed contracts going to organisations using zero hour contracts or the practice of blacklisting. SNP policy after independence is to establish a Fair Wage Commission to ensure that the minimum wage keeps up with inflation – but this would still be well below a 'living wage'.

6. The SNP passed a motion at its 2013 autumn conference to investigate the Commonweal idea. It gave no more commitment than that, highlighting that it may merely end up saying that it is already embodying the Commonweal idea when, in fact, to do so requires much more commitment to radical policies.

7. This makes the SWP's pamphlet, Scotland: Yes to independence, no to nationalism (SWP, 2012) a rather daft piece of ultra-leftism.

8. The reason why Canadian workers broke away from their international unions (i.e. North American unions) was that - with the bulk of membership of these unions in the USA – they believed that the domination of business unionism in the international unions and insufficient autonomy to the union jurisdictions in Canada were working against their interests.

9. Equally well, there remain a number of Scottish-only unions in teaching and NIPSA exists in the north of Ireland for public-sector workers. They are no less effective for being constituted in this way and are not accused of splitting the union movement or the working class. Members of the Scottish teaching unions and NIPSA took part in the 30 November 2011 pension strike.

10. If anything, one could hypothetically make the reverse argument, namely, that if union members in Scotland were freer to take further action – like after the 30 November 2011 pension strike – because they were not shackled by the restrictions and inhibitions of union leaderships like that of Unison, they were have been more action and a greater prospect of success.

Scotland the Brave?